Cloning

Other books in the Lucent Library of Science and Technology include:

Artificial Intelligence
Bacteria and Viruses
Black Holes
Comets and Asteroids
Computer Viruses
Energy Alternatives
Exploring Mars
Forensics
Genetics
Global Warming
The Internet
Lasers
Plate Tectonics
Space Stations
Telescopes
Virtual Reality

THE LUCENT LIBRARY OF SCIENCE AND TECHNOLOGY

Cloning

by Don Nardo

LUCENT BOOKS

An imprint of Thomson Gale, a part of The Thomson Corporation

THOMSON

★

GALE

Detroit • New York • San Francisco • San Diego • New Haven, Conn. • Waterville, Maine • London • Munich

LIBRARY OF CONGRESS CATALOGING-IN-PUBLICATION DATA

Nardo, Don, 1947–
   Cloning / by Don Nardo.
      p. cm. — (Lucent library of science and technology)
Includes bibliographical references and index.
ISBN 1-59018-773-3 (hard cover : alk. paper)
1. Cloning—Juvenile literature. I. Title. II. Series.
QH442.2.N373 2005
660.6'5—dc22

2005003521

Printed in the United States of America

Table of Contents

Foreword

"The world has changed far more in the past 100 years than in any other century in history. The reason is not political or economic, but technological—technologies that flowed directly from advances in basic science."

— Stephen Hawking, "A Brief History of Relativity," *Time*, 2000

The twentieth-century scientific and technological revolution that British physicist Stephen Hawking describes in the above quote has transformed virtually every aspect of human life at an unprecedented pace. Inventions unimaginable a century ago have not only become commonplace but are now considered necessities of daily life. As science historian James Burke writes, "We live surrounded by objects and systems that we take for granted, but which profoundly affect the way we behave, think, work, play, and in general conduct our lives."

For example, in just one hundred years, transportation systems have dramatically changed. In 1900 the first gasoline-powered motorcar had just been introduced, and only 144 miles (232km) of U.S. roads were hard-surfaced. Horse-drawn trolleys still filled the streets of American cities. The airplane had yet to be invented. Today 217 million vehicles speed along 4 million miles (6,437,376km) of U.S. roads. Humans have flown to the moon and commercial aircraft are capable of transporting passengers across the Atlantic Ocean in less than three hours.

The transformation of communications has been just as dramatic. In 1900 most Americans lived and worked on farms without electricity or mail delivery. Few people had ever heard a radio or spoken on a telephone. A hundred years later, 98 percent of American homes have telephones and televisions and more than 50 percent have personal computers. Some families even have more than one television and computer, and cell phones are now commonplace, even among the young. Data beamed from communication satellites routinely predict global weather conditions, and fiber-optic cable, e-mail, and the Internet have made worldwide telecommunication instantaneous.

Perhaps the most striking measure of scientific and technological change can be seen in medicine and public health. At the beginning of the twentieth century, the average American life span was forty-seven years. By the end of the century the average life span was approaching eighty years, thanks to advances in medicine including the development of vaccines and antibiotics, the discovery of powerful diagnostic tools such as X-rays, the lifesaving technology of cardiac and neonatal care, improvements in nutrition, and the control of infectious disease.

Rapid change is likely to continue throughout the twenty-first century as science reveals more about physical and biological processes such as global warming, viral replication, and electrical conductivity, and as people apply that new knowledge to personal decisions and government policy. Already, for example, an international treaty calls for immediate reductions in industrial and automobile emissions in response to studies that show a potentially dangerous rise in global temperatures is caused by human activity. Taking an active role in determining the direction of future changes depends on education; people must understand the possible uses of scientific research and the effects of the technology that surrounds them.

The Lucent Books Library of Science and Technology profiles key innovations and discoveries that have transformed the modern world. Each title strives to make a complex scientific discovery, technology, or phenomenon understandable and relevant to the reader. Because scientific discovery is rarely straightforward, each title explains the dead ends, fortunate accidents, and basic scientific methods by which the research into the subject proceeded. And every book examines the practical applications of an invention, branch of science, or scientific principle in industry, public health, and personal life, as well as potential future uses and effects based on ongoing research. Fully documented quotations, annotated bibliographies that include both print and electronic sources, glossaries, indexes, and technical illustrations are among the supplemental features designed to point researchers to further exploration of the subject.

Introduction

A New and Controversial Technology

For many people, cloning is a highly controversial technology. At the core of the debate over cloning lies its proposed use in projects involving human cells. Some people see much potential good in cloning these cells. Others worry that applying cloning technology to human cells might be unethical or destructive.

The Newness Factor

Putting the ethical considerations aside, human cloning is a relatively new concept. And a number of experts point out that, more than anything else, it is the newness factor that motivates much of the controversy. "Remarkable advances in science and technology," notes Princeton University scholar Lee M. Silver, often "force us to reconsider long-held notions of parenthood, childhood, and the meaning of life."[1] Cloning, he says, is one such advance.

Silver and others cite similar technologies that were controversial when they were new. There were widespread fears of heart transplants, for instance, when these operations first began in the mid–twentieth century. Some people believed that

A team of doctors performs heart-transplant surgery in 2002. When the procedure was first introduced, many people thought it violated God's wishes.

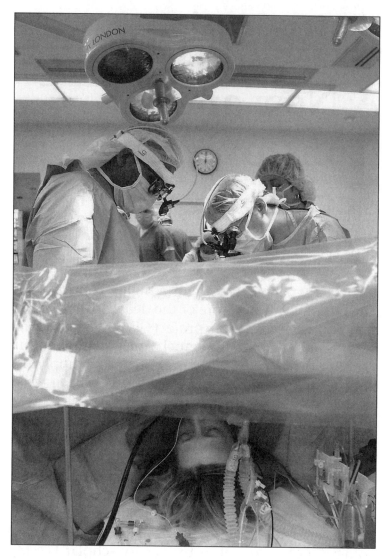

transplanting hearts was unnatural and against God's wishes and divine plan. Yet today heart transplants are widely accepted and save the lives of more than two thousand people a year.

Another parallel was the advent of in vitro fertilization (often called "test tube babies"). A number of religious leaders, politicians, and ordinary citizens said that this technique violated nature's and God's laws. Today, however, the technique is viewed as routine by the vast majority of people. And it produces between eleven and twelve thousand babies a year, allowing thousands of infertile couples to have biological children of their own.

In these and other cases, society as a whole was eventually able to overcome initial worries about a new technology. As long as scientists worked within certain guidelines and met certain social standards, most people came to accept ideas and techniques that at first had appeared strange, even scary. As one noted U.S. senator put it in 2002: "New science always brings new challenges and new debates. But we have proven in recent years that we can balance the promise of science with the ethical demands of our society."[2]

Cloning Now and in the Future

Experts on cloning also point out that the specific and controversial issue of human cloning has unfortunately tended to cloud the larger issue of cloning in general. This is because large numbers of people mistakenly equate human cloning with all cloning. Often they do not realize that the basic process of cloning is both nothing new and completely natural. The fact is that nature has been cloning plants and animals for hundreds of millions of years. And humans have been cloning plants for thousands of years without any fuss or controversy.

Indeed, huge amounts of the grains, vegetables, and fruits consumed around the world each year are clones. Moreover, animals of many different varieties are cloned routinely. In some ways, therefore, cloning is actually mundane.

Partly because many people are unaware that some types of cloning are routine, they are unfamiliar with the techniques involved. As a result, they lack a firm grasp of the technology. Indeed, Silver says, many people "are still confused about what the technology can and cannot do,"[3] either in reality now or potentially in the future.

Among the exciting potential uses for cloning, the experts say, is the production of medicines to help control genetic diseases such as hemophilia and cystic fibrosis. Parkinson's disease and other debilitating ailments may also be cured in the future through ingenious applications of cloning technology. Also, cloning techniques, combined with stem cells, another controversial emerging technology, show promise for growing human replacement organs. Many scientists are convinced that needy patients will be able to receive hearts, livers, kidneys, and other organs without fear of rejection by their immune systems. In addition, cloning technology will

In 2004 researchers in South Korea like these made a major breakthrough by cloning human embryos and harvesting stem cells from them.

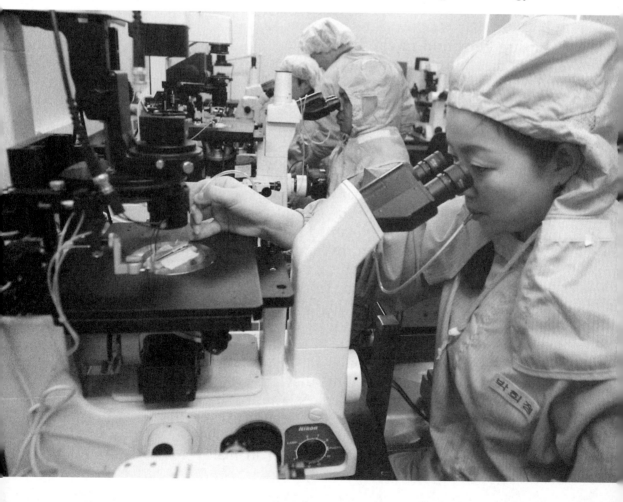

likely give infertile couples another way to have biological children of their own. Some scientists go so far as to predict a future in which some aspect of cloning technology will be an integral part of the lives of most people.

Even if cloning does become commonplace, at least some people may continue to feel uncomfortable with it. For them, the difference between cloning plants and animals and cloning human cells may always remain large and significant. Their moral arguments against human cloning cannot and should not be disregarded. Therefore, even when the newness factor of cloning wears off, it will likely be one area of scientific research that continues to raise eyebrows and arguments.

Chapter 1

Plant Cloning: From Nature to Agriculture

When most people hear the word *cloning* they think about scientists performing strange, complex experiments in laboratories in an effort to make duplicates of animals and human beings. Although such scientists and experiments do exist, they do not represent the main thrust of cloning in the world today. More than 99 percent of all cloning occurs in plants. Moreover, the vast majority of people are unaware that a large proportion of the plant products they buy—including fruits and vegetables—are clones. It is also not widely known that this practice is very ancient. Humans have been cloning plants for a long time, and nature has been doing it for even longer.

Nature's Clones

In fact, nature has been cloning plants (and animals too) for at least several hundred million years. On the simplest (and oldest) level, for instance, the very first living creatures on Earth—each of which consisted of a single cell—reproduced by cloning. No one knows exactly when and how these first living cells appeared. But abundant geologic evidence shows that they were thriving in large numbers in the oceans more than a billion years ago.

A brief examination of how these organisms reproduced conveniently provides a simple and concise definition for cloning in its most basic form. Two such cells did not need to get together to produce offspring (the sexual method, which most animals use today). Instead, each of these ancient, primitive cells utilized some of its own genetic material (more specifically its DNA, a complex chemical that contains the blueprints of life). Replication was therefore accomplished asexually, without the aid of another organism. The offspring of any living thing that reproduces by asexual means is a clone. Put simply, the parent, or genetic donor, passes on its DNA

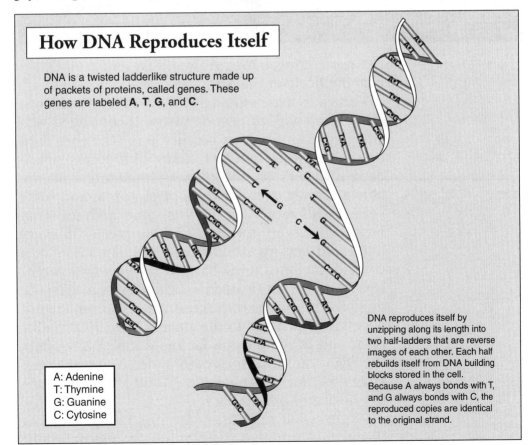

How DNA Reproduces Itself

DNA is a twisted ladderlike structure made up of packets of proteins, called genes. These genes are labeled **A**, **T**, **G**, and **C**.

A: Adenine
T: Thymine
G: Guanine
C: Cytosine

DNA reproduces itself by unzipping along its length into two half-ladders that are reverse images of each other. Each half rebuilds itself from DNA building blocks stored in the cell. Because A always bonds with T, and G always bonds with C, the reproduced copies are identical to the original strand.

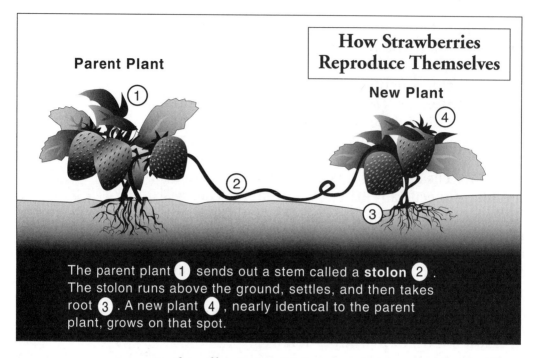

How Strawberries Reproduce Themselves

Parent Plant ①

New Plant ④

②

③

The parent plant ① sends out a stem called a **stolon** ②.
The stolon runs above the ground, settles, and then takes
root ③. A new plant ④, nearly identical to the parent
plant, grows on that spot.

to the offspring, which grows into a genetically identical duplicate of the parent.

This early mass cloning in the world's oceans was not a temporary or passing phase. It continued year after year, century after century, eon after eon, right up to the present. In fact, many of the most abundant microbes on the planet—including bacteria, blue-green algae, most kinds of protozoa, and some yeasts—still reproduce in this same manner. That means that every member of these species in every nook and cranny around the globe is a clone of a clone of a clone, going back to the very first parent DNA donors that floated in the ancient oceans. (The modern versions of these creatures, however, are not necessarily identical to the ancient ones. Heat, radiation, and other outside factors occasionally affect the DNA, causing a species to undergo tiny changes. Over time, such changes add up and alter the species to one degree or another.)

Single-celled organisms are not the only living things that undergo the cloning process naturally.

Some multicelled plants do so as well, including a number of familiar ones. For example, several types of ivy, a plant that creeps across the walls of university buildings far and wide, reproduce through cloning. So do vegetables such as artichokes, berries such as strawberries and blackberries, and garden flowers such as daffodils and tulips.

In the case of strawberries, each plant sends out a stem, called a stolon, above the ground. The stolon eventually settles down and takes root. Soon, a new strawberry plant grows in that spot, one that is genetically almost identical to the original plant. Daffodils, in contrast, clone by producing bulbs underground. The bulbs routinely produce clumps of new daffodils beside the originals, and the colony slowly spreads.

A more dramatic example of a plant that spreads through cloning is the water hyacinth. Like a strawberry plant, each hyacinth generates one or more narrow stems, each of which grows into an offspring that is genetically the same as the parent. Even more prolific than the strawberry, the hyacinth can spread rapidly through a given area, making it an irritating pest that can choke coastal waterways. "Away from its native habitat on the upper Amazon basin," says science writer Bijal Trivedi,

> the water hyacinth grows fast and spreads furiously, causing woes for man and beast. . . . [It] invaded the United States during the 19th century . . . [and] by the 1890s [it] already occupied the southeast coast of the U.S., infesting Florida, Texas, South Carolina, and Louisiana, which still has the biggest problem.[4]

Early Human Cloners

The fast-spreading water hyacinth dramatically demonstrates nature's expertise at cloning. This is perhaps not surprising considering that nature has

Fighting One of Nature's Toughest Clones

In this excerpt from an article for *National Geographic*'s online magazine, science writer Bijal Trivedi provides a brief overview of some efforts to stop the spread of one of nature's toughest and most efficient clones, the water hyacinth.

By the 1890s water hyacinth already occupied the southeast coast of the U.S., infesting Florida, Texas, South Carolina, and Louisiana, which still has the biggest problem. For decades man has fought the pest with an arsenal of more-or-less costly methods. Mechanical harvesters—a tugboat-mower—are slow. Herbicides are a quick fix, though with dangerous side effects. In the late 1960s, in South America, researchers discovered two weevils and a moth that destroy the water hyacinth. These creatures have been successfully released in more than 30 countries worldwide. In East Africa's Lake Victoria, for example, two weevil species reduced the coverage of water hyacinth by 80 percent. This conquest through biocontrol has spurred the search for other insects to match the range of climates where the water hyacinth thrives. . . . Using sweep nets . . . researchers collect insects and take them to a lab in Buenos Aires. There they test an insect to see whether it only has a taste for water hyacinth. Otherwise an introduction could threaten other indigenous species and some cash crops.

In Uganda, Africa, a worker clears away water hyacinths, which reproduce by cloning, from the waters of Lake Victoria.

had the benefit of more than a billion years of experimentation and practice. In comparison, humans are relative latecomers to the cloning process. The first cloning experiments by gardeners and farmers took place an estimated four thousand years ago in the Middle East (and possibly elsewhere).

The process these enterprising early horticulturists worked out, likely through trial and error, was fairly simple. A person took a twig or cutting from a plant and placed it in a container of earth. After roots started sprouting from the twig or cutting, he or she planted it in the ground. A few weeks later, the gardener had a new plant very similar to the original one. Over the course of generations, people learned that using cuttings from the strongest and healthiest plants increased the likelihood that any new plants would be strong and healthy. These ancient farmers had no idea *why* this process worked. After all, they possessed no knowledge of genes, DNA, or the scientific principles of cloning. All they knew was that taking the cuttings and planting them in a certain manner helped to ensure a good harvest.

This extremely useful knowledge continued to be passed from one generation to another. In addition, sometimes it was more than just the technique that people bequeathed to their descendants. In some areas of Europe, repeated cloning of a single strain of a crop kept the unique DNA blueprints of that strain alive for hundreds or even thousands of years. And in a few selected cases those strains survived to the present day. For example, among the many kinds of grapes used to make modern Italian wines are some that are clones of grapes that Roman farmers first grew in their vineyards more than two thousand years ago. The wine made from these grapes is almost identical, therefore, to the wine those ancient farmers, and perhaps a Roman emperor or two, drank in a dimly remembered age.

Modern Cloning for Food Production

Though lacking the venerable genetic heritage of ancient Roman grapes, numerous other fruits and vegetables widely consumed today are clones bearing DNA from long ago. One need go no farther than the local supermarket to find several examples. Particularly notable are the piles of apples in every market, each pile featuring specimens that are all roughly the same size, shape, and color. Someone with no knowledge of how apples are grown might suppose that this remarkable uniformity is the result of farmers using plenty of fertilizer, water, and tender loving care in their orchards. The reality is that the uniformity of the apples of a given type derives mainly from the fact that they are clones. They all possess almost identical DNA.

The farmers who grow the apples sold in modern supermarkets developed some varieties in the early to mid–twentieth century. However, a few popular apple species originated many years earlier. Cox's Orange Pippin apple, one of the most popular of all, is a good example. Every modern tree that produces this unique fruit is a clone of a single tree planted in one farmer's orchard early in the nineteenth century, almost two centuries ago.

Apples are not the only clones filling bins and shelves in modern markets. Several kinds of navel oranges are clones of a plump, juicy variety developed by a farmer in Southern California in the early years of the twentieth century. Similarly, a large proportion of Idaho potatoes are clones of a single potato plant grown in that state many decades ago. In fact, most potatoes harvested yearly around the world today are grown using basic cloning techniques. Some of these methods are explained by a spokesperson for Phytocultures Limited, a company that specializes in cloning potatoes and other crops:

The normal process for potato propagation [by cloning] is to grow a potato plant, and at the end of the season harvest the tubers that were produced during the growing season. Carefully store these tubers during the winter and in the spring plant the tubers in the ground. The resulting crop, barring environmental influences, will be identical to the potatoes produced in the previous year. . . . If we employ slightly more sophisticated methods, we can take cuttings from a Russet Burbank potato plant such as the upper portion of the stems, treat the stems with rooting powder and plant the stems in soil. The plant will grow and produce Russet Burbank potatoes.[5]

Most of the apples, oranges, and potatoes commonly found in supermarkets across the world are clones.

Some Advantages of Cloning Crops

Employing such cloning techniques to grow apples, oranges, potatoes, and other food crops has both advantages and disadvantages. One obvious advantage is that the apples or potatoes are more uniform and attractive, and therefore more appealing to the shoppers who see them in the stores. Using cloning, growers can also single out and perpetuate crop strains that taste better and/or are more nutritious.

In addition, cloning fruits and vegetables is more time-efficient and economical than more traditional methods. The time and money saved can benefit both the growers who produce and sell the food and the customers who buy and consume it. First consider the benefits for the farmers. By using cloning methods, they can maintain or manipulate the genes of their crops, creating either uniformity or controlled changes. So they are no longer at the mercy of the wide variation in quality that occurs when such crops grow naturally. Growers can rest assured that 90 percent or more of a given crop will be healthy and salable, whereas before it might have been only 60 to 70 percent (or less for some crops). Larissa Parsley, a journalist who investigates and monitors modern advances in farming, explains some of the strategies growers use to maintain such high crop yields:

A World-Famous Cloned Apple Tree

This tract published online by Common Ground, an English horticultural organization, describes the origins of the popular cloned apple known as Cox's Orange Pippin.

The most famous apple in the world was raised in Colnbrook [England] by Richard Cox, a retired brewer from Bermondsey. . . . In about 1825 [he] planted two seeds from a Ribston Pippin, which he is thought to have pollinated with a Blenheim Orange. Some years later, when the trees had fruited, he realized they had potential. These were later to be known as the Cox's Orange Pippin and Cox's Pomona. In 1836 he supplied some grafts to R. Small & Son, the local nurseryman . . . who sold the first trees in 1840. The varieties remained nationally unknown until Charles Turner, of the Royal Nurseries . . . started to promote them in 1850. The original Cox's Orange Pippin tree is thought to have blown down in a gale in 1911, but two sixty year old trees were seen still standing in the garden in 1933, presumably direct grafts from the original. Richard Cox died in 1845, aged 79, so he did not see the full fruits of his labor. Other nurserymen began to sell Cox's Orange Pippin trees and by 1883 it was already one of the most popular apples in the country. Now it is well known all over the world, and all the Cox's Orange Pippin trees ultimately derive from grafts from the original tree in Colnbrook.

A corn plant may be engineered in such a way so as to generate a certain protein that increases the efficiency of its growth cycle, therefore producing more corn in a shorter amount of time than the traditional corn plant. Another method of increasing crop yield is to confer resistance in plants normally damaged or destroyed by insects. A genetic modification may result in a new color pigment in the plant's leaves that wards off previously persistent insects, so that the plant is allowed to develop normally into a healthy source of food.[6]

These and other economic benefits of cloning various crops routinely help the customer as well. Because the grower's costs are less, he or she can pass part of the savings on to the consumer. Thus, higher crop yields that take less time and labor to produce often translate into lower prices in supermarkets.

Also, in the near future, according to experts, consumers will reap medical benefits from mass-produced crop clones. Working closely with selected farmers, in the past decade biologists and medical researchers have been trying to develop vaccines and antibiotics that can be engineered into the crops during the cloning process. Among these vaccines are edible ones, basically foods that contain agents that can fight or protect against disease. Such edible vaccines show promise for replacing some traditional immunization methods, such as injecting vaccines using needles. In fact, experiments are currently being performed to test the effectiveness of edible vaccines against the hepatitis B virus. In this regard, Parsley points out, cloned plants

also may be modified to work as "antibiotic factories," mass-producing bacterial antibiotics at a much faster rate than scientists can in a laboratory. An increased supply of antibiotics may

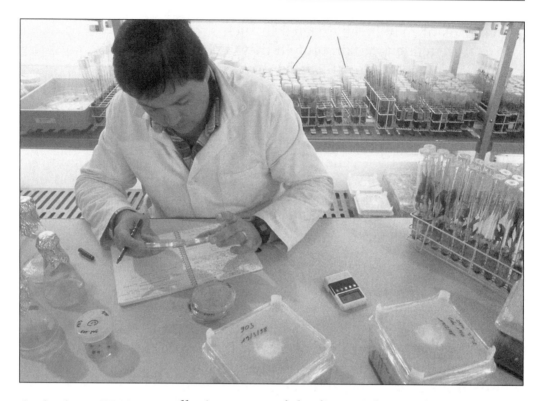

A scientist at CIRAD, an organization that conducts agricultural research, searches for improved ways to clone crops.

alleviate some of the financial struggles that consumers face against high-priced medications, and these genetic modifications may also lead to the development of new and more effective antibiotics. With our increasing knowledge of plant genetics and the techniques necessary to perform genetic modification, the possibilities seem endless. Plants can be cloned for study, be made to resist pesticides, and be modified to protect a child from contracting [certain diseases].[7]

Some Problems with Cloning Crops

But putting these benefits aside for the moment, what are the costs associated with producing food this way? The fact is that, as is the case with all forms of technology, cloning crops and other mass-produced plants has certain built-in problems and drawbacks. Farmers deal with these on a daily basis, while biologists work diligently to overcome them.

First and foremost among these problems is the practical reality that cloning plants is not a perfect and foolproof process. Contrary to popular opinion (often shaped by science fiction stories and movies), not all plant clones are identical to the original parent. And this can negatively affect both quality control and the size of the crop yield. Geneticist James F. Shepard explains:

Clones that differ in some obvious way from the parent [plant] sometimes appear. Such divergent individuals are called somatic variants, bud sports, or simply sports. They result from permanent genetic changes in specialized cells in the rapidly dividing cells at the tip of the growing stem, branch, or root that generate all or part of the new plant. Many important varieties of clonally propagated crop plants have arisen from such vegetative mutations. Famous examples are the pink grapefruit, the navel orange, the nectarine, and several varieties of potato. In other plants, for instance the sweet potato, sports appear with a frequency that can be as high as 2 percent. As a result, the maintenance of [genetic] purity [in a plant species] through conventional cloning is a continuing problem.[8]

Another problem that scientists and farmers face in producing crops through cloning is maintaining genetic diversity in order to ward off disease. Science has shown that plants that are genetically the same have the same vulnerability to certain diseases. Therefore, a disease that is fatal to a specific fruit or vegetable has a high probability of killing many or even all of its clones if it comes into contact with them. Hoping to prevent such a nightmare scenario, a number of farmers create multiple cloned lines of a single crop species. In other words, they breed two, three, or more slightly different varieties of a crop and then clone each of them. This strategy is based on the fact that most plant (as well as animal) diseases are highly selective and attack only one or a fairly limited number of species. Thus, if a grower has three cloned lines of potatoes and disease strikes one line, the potatoes in the other two lines may escape destruction. In this excerpt from an article for the *Washington Times*, noted science writer Keay Davidson uses a famous event to illustrate the problem and potential solution:

> One of history's worst disasters was the Irish potato famine of the early 19th century. It struck after the impoverished Irish grew dependent on a single variety of potato. When a potato disease wiped out the crop, hundreds of thousands of people died. Countless more fled to the New World. . . . If farmers continued growing a diversity of genetic types, they would have alternate breeds to fall back on during a potato famine–type crisis.[9]

Though this strategy is widely acknowledged to be a wise and effective one, several experts say that it is not employed nearly as often as it should be. In fact, they warn, far too few American farmers are presently growing multiple cloned lines to guard against plant epidemics. According to Davidson, if a potent disease unexpectedly strikes a given farming region, an entire crop of clones with identical DNA might be wiped out. Calling for more genetic diversity, as well as government regulation to ensure it, Davidson writes:

> [Genetic] diversity [in cloned crops] has waned over the past century in the United States. 91 percent of the different breeds of corn have disappeared, along with 95 percent of the varieties of cabbage, 94 percent of peas, 86 percent of ap-

ples, and 81 percent of tomatoes. . . . What's the solution? The White House should at least declare a "moral commitment" to genetic diversity in agriculture. Working with Congress, it could come up with financial incentives to encourage farmers to enrich their genetic harvest—say, by raising more than one type of corn.[10]

Crop cloners must be careful to guard against plant diseases. Here, a grower holds up grapes infected by Pierce's Disease next to some healthy ones.

"Invasion of the Forest Snatchers"

Disease is only one of the problems posed by lack of diversity in mass-produced cloned crops. Implantation of such a crop on an unusually large scale, along with failure to diversify, can have a ripple effect that can cause a wide array of environmental and economic troubles. Just such a worrisome scenario is presently unfolding in Argentina. Since the mid-1990s, that country's agricultural system has come to be dominated by a single crop (although other crops are grown there on a much smaller scale). That crop is a cloned, genetically engineered strain of soybean developed by an American company. So far, some 34 million acres (13,759,312 hectares) of Argentine land have been devoted to the plant.

An Argentine farmer holds some of his cloned soybeans, which some experts worry are susceptible to disease.

Critics in Argentina, the United States, Europe, and elsewhere point out that the whole soybean crop in Argentina is susceptible to collapse if an unexpected disease strikes. But beyond this danger, they say, are several others. First, these cloned soybeans are resistant to most common herbicides. So local farmers must use more powerful herbicides more often to keep pests away. This encourages the growth of herbicide-resistant weeds and degrades (removes nutrients from) the soil.

In turn, following the ripple effect, degraded soil produces fewer and less hardy plants. As a result, farmers find that they must plant more of the cloned soybeans in newer soil, which necessitates cutting down forests to create fresh farmland. The rate of deforestation in Argentina is now three to six times the average in the rest of the world. Up to 50 percent of the country's wild animal species, which live in these forests, will be potentially threatened in the next few decades. It is no wonder that Greenpeace and other pro-environmental organizations have come to call the situation the "invasion of the forest snatchers." (This is a reference to the popular 1950s horror film *Invasion of the Body Snatchers*, in which aliens use large seed pods in an attempt to clone emotionless duplicates of human beings.)

Although the United States and Argentina have been singled out here, the problem is global. At the moment, many farmers in nations around the world do not diversify their cloned food crops. They appear to feel that, despite decreasing genetic diversity, the potential huge advantages of cloning crops outweigh the potential disadvantages. Only time will tell if this risk is worth taking. In the meantime, scientists continue to experiment with new ways of applying one of nature's most important inventions—cloning—to agriculture.

Chapter 2

The First Cloned Animals

When growing food by artificial cloning became a big business in the twentieth century, many scientists reasoned that the next logical step would be to clone domestic animals. In this view, mass cloning of cattle, sheep, pigs, and chickens would be an efficient way of creating larger, healthier, more valuable herds and flocks. For example, a farmer who raised cows would be able to choose the cows that gave the most milk and produce whole herds of them. Cloning animals would also aid laboratory researchers who have a regular need for various kinds of animals for experiments and tests. Usually they prefer that all the lab animals in a test be as much alike as possible to be sure that physical and other differences in the animals do not affect and confuse the results.

As these researchers discovered, however, cloning animals turned out to be a great deal more difficult than cloning plants. Before attempting to clone mammals such as sheep, scientists tried to clone frogs, which are, physically speaking, much less complex and sophisticated than mammals. These experiments failed. So for a while, a majority of researchers became pessimistic about animal cloning, viewing it as too difficult to accomplish with existing technology. However, over the years technology steadily improved. This inspired a few daring scientists to try animal cloning again, and eventually they were successful.

Many Early Failures

The reasons for the eventual success of animal cloning can readily be seen by a brief examination of why the earlier attempts to achieve this difficult goal failed. In the 1930s Nobel prize–winning biologist Hans Spemann suggested a way that an animal might be cloned. First, he said, one could remove an egg from a female animal. The next step is to remove the genetic material from the nucleus of the egg and replace it with the genetic material from a cell of the animal one wants to reproduce through cloning. In time, said Spemann, the egg will grow into an embryo. When it does, one should implant it into the uterus of a female of the species, and in a few months a cloned offspring will be born.

One benefit of cloning cows is the ability to reproduce large numbers of healthy cattle with high milk-producing capacity.

In the 1930s Nobel Prize–winning biologist Hans Spemann suggested a way to clone animals.

This was, and remains, the basic theory behind animal cloning. As every scientist knows, however, theory is one thing and actual practice is often quite another. When Spemann tried to apply these seemingly simple steps to salamanders and other amphibians, he failed repeatedly. Eventually, he abandoned the research.

Though Spemann had reached what he considered a dead end, some younger scientists believed that he had been basically on the right track. About twenty years later, in the 1950s, Robert Briggs and Thomas J. King, both of Philadelphia's Institute for Cancer Research, attempted to follow the same steps Spemann had laid out for the animal cloning process. With great difficulty, they managed to remove the nucleus from a frog's egg and replace it with the nucleus from a cell taken from the tissue of a frog. The result was a cloned frog embryo. But this embryo quickly died, as did many similar ones that Briggs and King created in succeeding months. In the 1960s other researchers repeated these experiments with similar results.

Looking back at these early experiments in animal cloning, modern scientists understand fully why they did not work. In a nutshell, the lab equipment available to Spemann, Briggs, King, and the others was not nearly intricate and delicate enough to accomplish the microscopic work involved. During the experiments, the clumsy instruments (by modern standards) damaged the genetic material of the eggs and cells, so they could not grow normally. And any embryos created were flawed from the start and doomed to die.

The Problem of Differentiated Cells

There was also another difficulty that the early animal cloning researchers had to overcome, one that had nothing to do with the quality of their instruments. This problem was related to the fundamental differences between embryonic, or immature, cells and adult, or mature, cells. The theory behind cloning seemed to indicate that one placed the genetic material

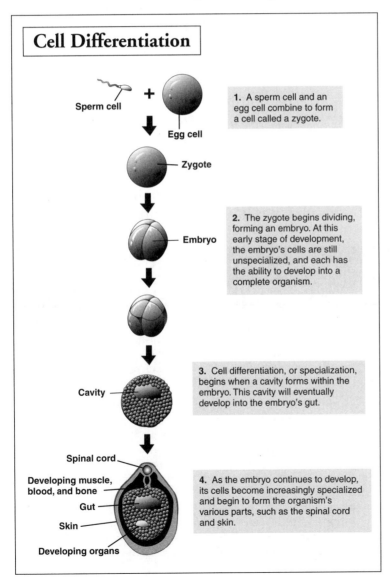

Cell Differentiation

Sperm cell

+

Egg cell

1. A sperm cell and an egg cell combine to form a cell called a zygote.

Zygote

Embryo

2. The zygote begins dividing, forming an embryo. At this early stage of development, the embryo's cells are still unspecialized, and each has the ability to develop into a complete organism.

Cavity

3. Cell differentiation, or specialization, begins when a cavity forms within the embryo. This cavity will eventually develop into the embryo's gut.

Spinal cord

Developing muscle, blood, and bone

Gut

Skin

Developing organs

4. As the embryo continues to develop, its cells become increasingly specialized and begin to form the organism's various parts, such as the spinal cord and skin.

from an adult cell into the nucleus of an embryonic cell to create the desired cloned embryo. But for a long time it appeared to be too difficult, perhaps even impossible, to clone from an adult cell. The scientists wondered why this was so.

Some researchers suspected that the reason for this difficulty was connected to a phenomenon of normal cell and tissue growth called differentiation. "Every cell in the body arises from the same fertilized egg and so every cell in the body has exactly the same genes," noted science writer Gina Kolata explains.

But animal—and human—cells are specialized, differentiated, so that a heart cell behaves like a heart cell and a liver cell like a liver cell. The process of differentiation begins almost as soon as a fetus forms, and once a cell has reached its final state, it never alters. A brain cell remains a brain cell for as long as a person is alive; it never

The Motivation Behind Dolly's Creation

In her book *Clone: The Road to Dolly and the Path Ahead*, science writer Gina Kolata summarizes the motivation behind the Roslin Institute's efforts to clone sheep, namely the desire to create herds of animals that might produce pharmaceutical drugs in an economical, efficient manner.

> [Such sheep] might produce valuable drugs much more cheaply than did the methods used by drug companies. . . . [The researchers] would clone a lamb whose udder cells made the drug whenever they made milk—all they'd have to do is hook the drug-producing gene to the gene that is turned on when milk is produced and make clones from those genetically altered cells. Then the company could simply milk the sheep, extract the drug from the milk, and sell it. If the scientists made both male and female sheep that carried the added gene, they could breed these sheep and have a self-perpetuating flock of living drug factories.

turns into a liver cell, even though its genes are the same.[11]

Thus, the experiments in animal cloning performed before the 1980s seemed to show that primitive cloning of embryonic cells was possible. However, once the cells had become differentiated, or specialized, the cloning process broke down and became impractical, perhaps even impossible.

Enter Ian Wilmut and the Roslin Institute

Still, a handful of enterprising researchers became convinced that they could somehow overcome these technical obstacles. Among them was embryologist Ian Wilmut, who headed a team of scientists at the Roslin Institute, in Roslin, Scotland. The Roslin labs had been established during World War II when Britain was suffering from severe war-related food shortages. The institute's original purpose was to exploit the then new and promising field of genetics to produce more food from existing resources. In the decades that followed the war, the Roslin labs redirected their efforts to finding ways of making standard livestock, including cattle, sheep, and pigs, healthier and more productive.

It was this desire to increase the productivity of domestic animals that motivated Wilmut and his colleagues to begin experimenting with animal cloning in 1986. More specifically, the researchers wanted to find more effective ways of using sheep to make drugs that might help fight human diseases. In particular, the targets were hemophilia (in which the blood does not clot properly, increasing the chances of a person bleeding to death) and cystic fibrosis (a glandular disorder that causes severe respiratory distress).

In this regard, the Roslin team was to some degree building on the work of other scientists. Other labs had earlier discovered a way to genetically engineer sheep so that their milk contained a drug called alpha-1 antitrypsin. Because this drug had shown considerable promise in treating cystic fibrosis, it would be very beneficial and valuable. The problem, Wilmut and his colleagues realized, was that only a small quantity of alpha-1 antitrypsin can be extracted from the milk of a single sheep. Moreover, the steps needed to make even a few sheep produce the drug were extremely time-consuming and expensive.

This led Wilmut and the others to think about cloning sheep as a more economically viable alternative. Their reasoning went as follows: If they could take a cell from an adult sheep that had already been genetically altered to produce the drug and clone that cell, all of the sheep's offspring would be automatically programmed to produce the drug. In that way, any and all of the sheep that were cloned might become in a sense living drug factories. Researchers could theoretically clone a lamb that produced milk containing the drug; create hundreds or thousands of identical offspring, each of which also produced milk containing the drug; and finally, simply milk the sheep and extract the drug from the milk.

The First Cloned Mammals

This scenario certainly seemed logical and doable on paper. In practice, however, as Wilmut and his team fully realized, it was going to be very difficult. So far, no one had managed to clone healthy living animals from any kind of cell, much less an adult, fully differentiated cell.

For this reason, Wilmut and one of his colleagues, biologist Keith Campbell, decided they were not ready to try cloning with a cell taken directly from a live animal. Instead, it seemed to make more sense to start by cloning a mammal from a cell extracted from an embryo grown in the lab under strictly controlled conditions. It was important to make sure that the embryo's cells had already become differentiated because all later experiments with live animals would involve differentiated cells.

But how could they extract the DNA they needed from a differentiated cell? The results of all previous experiments had suggested that it was not possible to clone from such cells. It was Campbell who came up with the brilliant idea of slowing down the cellular activity of a differentiated embryonic cell so that it would react more like a younger, undifferentiated embryonic cell. As Campbell himself explained in a later interview, this was accomplished by making the cell become quiescent, or go to sleep:

> If a cell can be made to enter an inactive state called quiescence, in which there is no growth occurring and DNA replication has not occurred, we can perform nuclear transfer [i.e., cloning]. We achieved quiescence by depriving cells . . . of needed nutrients. [The result was that] few if any genes remained switched on. When their nuclei were removed, placed next to

Dr. Ian Wilmut of the Roslin Institute headed the team that produced the world's first cloned sheep.

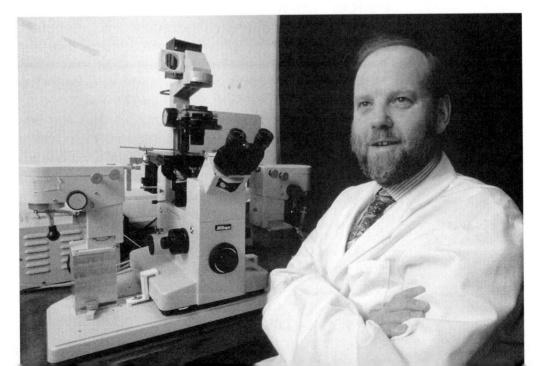

Pictured here are the identical faces of Megan and Morag, the first mammals cloned from lab-grown embryos.

egg cells, and fused [to the egg cells] by an electric current, the eggs were able to reprogram the donor nuclei so that they behaved as if they came from an undifferentiated cell.[12]

This revolutionary experiment, which took place early in 1995, resulted in the successful creation of two new embryos. These grew normally until Campbell, Wilmut, and the others implanted them into the wombs of some adult female sheep. Not long afterward, in August of that year, two lambs were born. The Roslin team named them Megan and Morag.

Today it may seem somewhat odd that the creation of the world's first cloned mammals was barely noticed by the press and public. Except for a few interested scientists, no one paid much attention to the article published in the prestigious scientific journal *Nature* in which Wilmut and Campbell described their achievement. Looking at these events in retrospect, the lack of public interest may have come from the fact that the Roslin researchers had not actually cloned a living animal. The cells used to clone Megan and Morag had come from embryos grown in the lab.

Dolly Creates a Sensation

To Wilmut, Campbell, and their colleagues, the crucial lesson of the creation of Megan and Morag was that they had proven beyond a doubt that differentiated cells could be cloned. The next obvious step was to use the techniques they had developed to clone a cell taken from a living adult mammal. In Ian Wilmut's own words:

> In the Winter of 1995–1996, Keith [Campbell and our colleagues proceeded] . . . to clone lambs from . . . cultures derived from adult mammary gland cells. . . . In the most important respects, the method was the one that we [had used] for Megan and Morag. We deprived the cultured cells of growth factor [i.e., nutrients] for five days to put them into the quiescent [hibernating] state. . . . [We] constructed 277 embryos from the . . . mammary cells. . . . Twenty-nine of them successfully developed into [larger, more advanced embryos]. These were transferred into [the wombs of] thirteen ewes [female sheep], of which one [belonging to the Scottish Blackface sheep breed] became pregnant; and this solitary Scottish Blackface surrogate mother went on to produce a live Finn-Dorset lamb.[13]

The Roslin scientists named the little lamb Dolly. Though excited by and proud of their achievement, they did not announce her existence right away. This was mainly because they first needed to do some genetic tests to make sure that no mistakes had been made—that Dolly had indeed grown from a cell taken from an adult sheep. These tests proved positive. The researchers also had to take the time to describe what they had done in writing. Finally, they announced their accomplishment in the February 1997 issue of *Nature*.

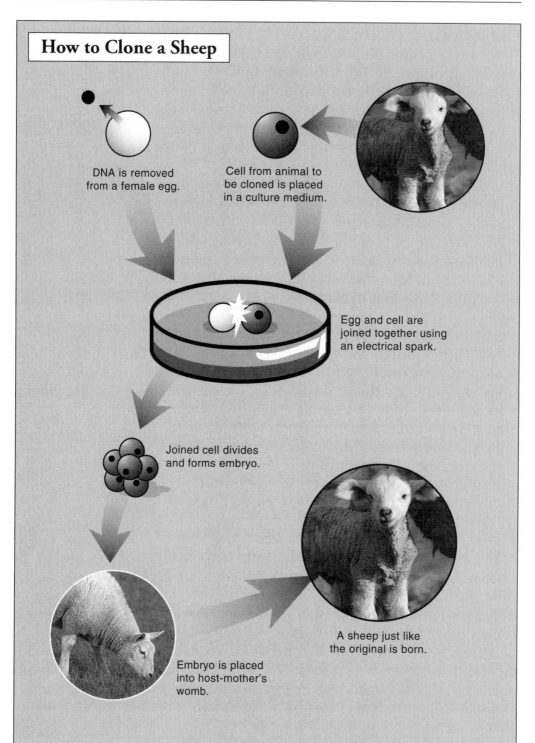

How to Clone a Sheep

DNA is removed from a female egg.

Cell from animal to be cloned is placed in a culture medium.

Egg and cell are joined together using an electrical spark.

Joined cell divides and forms embryo.

Embryo is placed into host-mother's womb.

A sheep just like the original is born.

Whereas public reactions to the birth of Megan and Morag had been almost nonexistent, the news of Dolly's creation became an overnight, worldwide sensation. The Roslin scientists found themselves overwhelmed by what seemed like a flood of interest in what they had done. In the first five days immediately following the announcement of Dolly's birth, the institute received more than two thousand telephone calls and had to deal directly with almost a hundred newspaper reporters, sixteen film crews, and more than fifty professional photographers. Meanwhile, Dolly became front-page news in nearly every newspaper and news magazine in the world.

Wilmut and his fellow researchers were particularly struck by one aspect included in a majority of the articles, reports, talk show segments, and other coverage of Dolly and the process that had created her. Namely, most of the media and public interest focused very little on animal cloning itself and its potential uses. Instead, nearly everyone seemed obsessed with where this new technology might lead. If an animal as sophisticated as a sheep could be cloned, most commentators said, human cloning could well be the next step.

There were two basic and almost polar opposite reactions to Dolly's birth, therefore. Some people were excited and

A symbolic double image of Dolly is featured on the cover of the March 10, 1997, issue of Time.

optimistic, saying that the achievement of the Roslin scientists showed that there might be no limits to what science could accomplish in the future. In contrast, many other people found the news of Dolly's creation disturbing. They worried that cloning technology might somehow tamper in God's domain and therefore was an area humans should stay out of.

The degree to which Dolly's birth got people thinking about the ethics of cloning—whether they agreed with it or not—was illustrated by the sudden popularity of bioethicists, scholars who study and make judgments about whether certain aspects of scientific research are ethical or not. Before the Dolly controversy, the Internet Web site operated by Arthur Caplan, director of the Center for Bioethics at the University of Pennsylvania, received about five hundred hits a month. In the weeks following Dolly's birth, that number jumped to more than seventeen thousand per day.

The Stuff That Makes Myths

Ian Wilmut and the other members of the Roslin team were proud of their accomplishment, and rightly so, for it marked a major milestone in the history of science. Wilmut himself later wrote about it in his book *The Second Creation*.

Dolly has one startling attribute that is forever unassailable [beyond question]. She was the first animal of any kind to be created from cultured, differentiated cells taken from an *adult*. Thus she confutes [disproves] once and for all the notion—virtual dogma for 100 years—that once cells are committed to the tasks of adulthood, they cannot again be [capable of supplying the genetic material for creating another life]. The cell that created Dolly came from an adult ewe—indeed, the ewe that provided her genes was almost elderly—yet its ability to be reprogrammed into [the capacity to create a new lamb] was demonstrated beyond question. . . . All and all, Dolly is the stuff of which myths are made. Her birth was otherworldly, literally a virgin birth or, at least, one that did not result directly from an act of sex.

From Pigs to Flies

Whether the general public thought that cloning higher animals was right or wrong did not matter much to scientists like Ian Wilmut or to the heads of big farming businesses and drug companies. These individuals immediately recognized the economic potential of mass-cloning sheep, cattle, and other mammals. After all, it had been the desire to create "living drug factories" that had motivated the Roslin researchers in the first place.

Not surprisingly, therefore, right after the announcement of Dolly's creation, scientific teams around the world—many of them funded by big business—began trying to clone animals. Between 1997 and 2003, cattle, horses, goats, pigs, mice, rabbits, and cats were all successfully cloned. Most of these animals were created using the same basic technology the Roslin researchers had employed in making Dolly (although a few were cloned from embryonic rather than adult cells). Also, the vast majority were born to surrogate mothers (instead of the animals that had donated the cells for the cloning procedures).

In fact, this is what made the first cloned horse so unusual. It was the first cloned mammal that was carried to term by the mother that had donated the cell for the cloning procedure. The baby horse, named Prometea, was born in May 2003, the result of a cloning success by scientists at the Lab of Reproductive Technology in Cremona, Italy. According to Patricia Reaney, the reporter who broke the story:

Named after Prometheus, who in Greek mythology was punished for stealing fire from the gods and giving it to humans, the foal was created through nuclear transfer—the same technique used for Dolly the sheep, the world's first cloned mammal. [The Italian] team removed a skin cell

This August 2003 photo shows the world's first cloned horse, Prometea (left), and her mother and genetic twin, Stella.

from the mother and fused it to an egg from which the nucleus had been removed. After the activated egg was grown in the laboratory it was replaced in the horse from which it had been cloned. The scientists started out with more than 800 manipulated eggs using male and female cells. Twenty-two developed into seven-day-old embryos and 17 were transferred into nine horses. Four pregnancies resulted but Prometea was the only live animal.[14]

Other such cloning successes followed. In the same year that Prometea came into the world, French and Chinese researchers cloned rats for the first time. And also that same year scientists at the University of Idaho produced the first clone of a hybrid mammal, in this case a mule (a cross between a horse and a donkey). Moreover, mammals were not the only creatures created in this veritable explosion of animal cloning. In November 2004 scientists at

Dalhousie University in Nova Scotia, Canada, announced that they had successfully cloned fruit flies.

Dolly's Demise and the Future

In the meantime, all of these success stories were overshadowed somewhat by the news that Dolly the sheep—the first mammal ever to be cloned from a living creature—had died on February 14, 2003, at the age of six. (Normal life spans for sheep range from six to twelve years.) More accurately, her creators had put her to sleep to keep her from suffering. Dolly had developed a serious infection in her lungs and painful arthritis in many of her joints.

The question on every researcher's mind was whether the ailments Dolly had developed were caused by the cloning process that had created her. So far, the evidence is inconclusive. On the one hand, studies of her chromosomes (the chains of genes found in each cell) showed that their ends, called telomeres, were slightly shorter than in average sheep. However, Dolly had four offspring (including Bonnie, born in 1998, and three other lambs born in 1999), and tests showed that the telomeres of these sheep are perfectly normal. Much more research will have to be done to determine whether the cloning process inevitably causes abnormalities in animals.

But whether the cloning process hastened Dolly's death or not, the pace of animal cloning is not likely to slow. Thousands of labs and farms around the world are presently cloning animals of various kinds. The race is definitely on to transform animal cloning into a multibillion-dollar enterprise, a goal expected to be attained no later than the year 2012. Financial backers of these endeavors cite a host of benefits they claim that humanity will reap—from increased food production, to cheaper production of medicinal drugs, to the creation of transplant organs for both animals and humans.

Chapter 3

Potential Advantages of Cloning Animals

The creation of Dolly, the first animal cloned from a cell taken from a living adult animal, was not merely a big news story. It marked the beginning of an entirely new area of scientific endeavor, as well as a new and potentially profitable large-scale industry—practical animal cloning. Companies and labs around the world immediately followed the lead of the Roslin Institute scientists and began cloning animals. In particular, they concentrated their efforts on creating domesticated farm and lab animals through cloning. Late in 1997, for example, researchers at a Wisconsin company, Infigen, cloned a bull, which they named Gene. By early 2001, the company had successfully cloned more than a hundred cattle, and in 2002 it cloned several pigs from cells taken from adult pigs.

Companies like Infigen claim that their goal is to use cloning to aid the farming industry. Entire herds of genetically engineered animals can be created, they say, giving farmers the benefit of more healthy, productive animals. Spokespeople for these companies admit that cloning is still a complex and expensive process. So it will be a few years before such

46

herds of cloned animals can be manufactured cheaply enough to be economically viable for an average dairy or beef farmer. However, the companies are confident that within a few years interested farmers will be able to scan catalogues listing available cloned livestock embryos. They will be able to choose the embryos they desire, order them by phone or the Internet, and then implant them in the wombs of some of their existing cows, pigs, or sheep.

Other potential benefits of animal cloning include medical ones, for both animals and humans. Scientists are already able to genetically alter certain animals to make them more resistant to some diseases. If such a disease-resistant animal is cloned, in theory the result might be a whole herd of animals, each of which is less likely to contract one or more illnesses. This same technology might also be extended to bring medical benefits to humans. Useful drugs and effective medicines might be extracted from cloned herds of genetically altered animals. Also, cloned animals might contribute organs that in some cases could be transplanted into humans whose own organs are failing.

In 1997 these rhesus monkeys were cloned from embryos at the Oregon Regional Primate Research Center.

Creating Healthier Animals

Researchers admit that before cloning animals becomes a realistic way to make people healthier, they must first demonstrate that cloning can be used to make animals healthier. For farmers who raise livestock, the prospect of reducing the incidence of certain animal diseases is certainly attractive. Various illnesses affect cows, pigs, chickens, and other livestock every year, reducing productivity and costing farmers a great deal of money.

Mastitis, a bacterial inflammation of the udders of cows, is a good example. An estimated one-quarter to one-third of dairy cows are afflicted with mastitis at one time or another. While they are sick, the cows either have trouble producing milk or produce milk that is significantly lower in quality than that given

Cloning holds the potential of reducing the incidence of animal diseases, such as mastitis, which affects dairy cows.

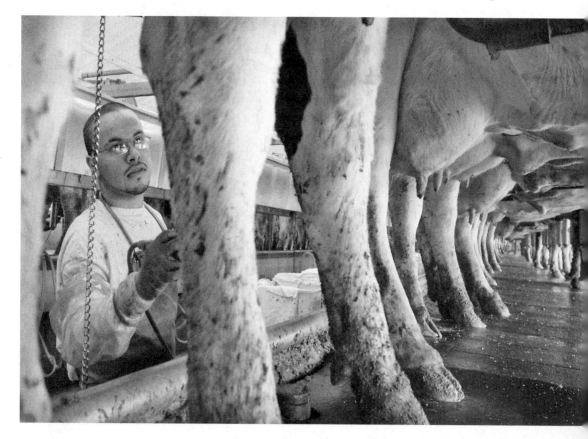

by healthy cows. According to a spokesperson for the University of Tennessee Institute of Agriculture, mastitis

> causes billions of dollars annually in lost revenue to the dairy industry due to lost production, investments in animal care, poor reproductive performance, and milk that has to be discarded. This results in higher consumer costs for dairy products.[15]

In an effort to reduce the incidence of mastitis and other diseases of livestock, the University of Tennessee launched the University of Tennessee Cloning Project. "We are attempting to establish the genetic relationship of mastitis susceptibility,"[16] said one of the leaders of the project. In other words, the scientists are attempting to find out to what extent the disease is caused or affected by genetic factors. Defective genes might then be altered or eliminated, decreasing the negative effects of mastitis. "The overall goal of this research effort," states Dr. Steve Oliver, a University of Tennessee food safety expert, "is to enhance the quantity, quality and safety of milk and meat produced by dairy cows while simultaneously increasing farmer profitability."[17]

The university's cloning team achieved an impressive initial success in October 2002 with the births of ten calves cloned from a single Jersey cow. That cow was suffering from a chronic case of mastitis, and the researchers wanted to determine if the disease could be passed from one generation to the next through defective genes. Since both the donor cow and all of its offspring have the same DNA, cloning affords a unique opportunity to study both the genes and the disease under highly simplified and controlled conditions. (Having the infected cow mate with a bull to produce the offspring for the study would add complications such as the bull's

DNA and overall health.) Assessing the achievement of the cloned calves and the overall potential of the project's research, Oliver concludes:

> The clones may be invaluable for determining potential genes, immune components, and other factors associated with and responsible for mastitis resistance. Identifying these factors could lead to improved animal selection strategies and novel approaches for eradicating or reducing diseases of food-producing animals.[18]

Cloning to Combat Human Diseases

Researchers are also making progress in using animal cloning to help fight diseases that affect humans. Scientists are pursuing several strategies, one of which was the underlying motivation for the Roslin Institute's creation of Dolly. Ian Wilmut and his colleagues set out to make it easier and less expensive to produce large quantities of alpha-1 antitrypsin (AAT). This potent drug has for some time been used to treat cystic fibrosis, as well as emphysema, another disease that impairs the normal functioning of the lungs and causes severe shortness of breath. "Emphysema affects 100,000 people a year in Europe and North America alone," Wilmut says in a brief overview of the two ailments.

> The underlying cause is a genetic defect that leads to AAT deficiency. Cystic fibrosis is the most common single-gene disorder among Caucasians. An astonishing one person in twenty carries the defective gene, and one in 1,600 inherits this mutant gene in a double dose and then suffers from the disease. . . . The normal task of AAT is to counteract the effects of [an] enzyme, elastase, in the lungs. Elastase keeps the lungs flexible, but if it is not brought to a halt when its work is done, it attacks the

lung tissue. In cystic fibrosis and emphysema, elastase does get out of control.[19]

Doctors have shown that AAT can be effective in partially restoring normal lung function in patients with cystic fibrosis and emphysema. The problem has always been the difficulty and expense of producing the drug. Before animal cloning became a reality, AAT was taken from human blood plasma in the laboratory, an approach plagued by a number of disadvantages. First, the procedures involved are very expensive. Also, the use of blood plasma to extract such drugs diminishes the already limited supplies of blood needed for transfusions. Another potential problem is that using blood plasma in this manner can be risky because some human blood supplies are presently contaminated by diseases such as hepatitis and AIDS.

Extracting pharmaceutical drugs from cloned animals eliminates these problems. Experts point out that herds of cloned sheep could be "pharmed" to

This Jersey calf, named Millie, was born via the cloning process in 2000. Entire herds of cloned cattle were eventually created.

produce supplies of AAT that are cheaper and safer and that will free up the blood supply for transfusion and other purposes. (*Pharming*, meaning the farming of drugs, is a relatively new term that combines the words *farming* and *pharmaceutical*.)

Hemophilia is another disease that might be combated by pharming cloned animals. For a person with hemophilia, the blood does not clot properly. The disease is caused by a genetic defect, specifically a lack of the gene that orders the body to make factors VIII and IX, the proteins that cause the blood to clot. Because one or both of these factors are missing from a hemophiliac's blood, he or she can suffer significant blood loss from a cut that would be a mere nuisance to the average person. Hemophiliacs are usually treated by receiving transfusions of blood that contains the missing clotting factor or factors. However, the positive effects of such transfusions are not permanent because the human body routinely makes new blood. In a hemophiliac, this new blood, which lacks the clotting factors, steadily replaces the transfused blood that contains the clotting factors.

In theory, this problem could be eliminated by the pharming of cloned animals. Certain animals could

Can Pharming Cloned Animals Help Diabetics?

A number of researchers say that the same cloning strategies and techniques that may help hemophiliacs also show promise for producing insulin, a hormone used in the treatment and control of diabetes. This condition, which affects one in twenty people in the United States, is characterized by decreased production of insulin by the pancreas and unwanted increases of sugar and other substances in the bloodstream. Many diabetics must take doses of insulin daily to avoid serious illness or even death. Cloning herds of animals that have been genetically altered to produce insulin would make it much faster and cheaper to manufacture the hormone than is possible using present laboratory methods. This would, in turn, make the insulin far more affordable for diabetics.

be genetically altered to produce the clotting factors VIII and IX in their milk. Then the clotting factors could be separated from the milk (a fairly easy process) for use in treating hemophiliacs.

Between 1998 and 2002, a number of companies began gearing up to carry out such pharmaceutical drug pharming on a mass scale. Among these efforts were the early stages of creating herds of transgenic cows capable of producing unusually large amounts of milk. (The term *transgenic* refers to an animal that has been altered to carry the genes of one or more other species besides its own.) Among the early leaders in the race to clone and pharm animals for medical purposes were PPL Therapeutics, based in Scotland; Genzyme Transgenics, in Massachusetts; Advanced Cell Technology, also in Massachusetts; Pharming Holding, in the Netherlands; and ABS Global, in Wisconsin.

Unexpected Difficulties with Pharming

These and other companies invested huge sums of money in initial research and development. They expected that costs would be high at first, but were confident that future profits would be even higher and would therefore offset these start-up costs. As often happens during the initial stages of all new technologies, however, unexpected problems arose that further increased research and development costs. Some of the problems were highly technical in nature. Though the researchers involved were confident they could overcome the difficulties, projected production schedules slowed considerably. For example, some companies initially thought they could begin harvesting AAT from herds of cloned animals by 2005. That goal had to be put off to 2007 and then to 2009. One result was that some of the financial backers involved began to doubt they would make a profit.

Other setbacks occurred in 2002 and 2003 when press releases revealed that Dolly had developed first

The world's first cloned pigs—Noel, Angel, Star, Joy, and Mary—were born on Christmas Day in 2001.

premature arthritis and then debilitating lung problems. There was (and remains) no definite proof that the cloning process had caused Dolly's ailments. Nevertheless, public perceptions were shaped in large degree by fears that cloning might be the culprit. Groups that lobby for the humane treatment of animals voiced concerns that the animals in the growing cloned herds might be suffering needless pain. This created still more bad press, which in turn increased the worries of some financial investors in the big pharming ventures.

As a result of these and other related problems, leaders of the pharming industry reluctantly began to scale back their efforts in 2002 and 2003. In 2003, for instance, after its main financial backers withdrew their support, PPL had no choice but to have many of its cloned sheep humanely put to sleep. The following year PPL, once one of the leaders in the new pharming industry, filed for bankruptcy. Investigator Mike Adcock, of the BBC (British Broadcasting Corporation), gives this general assessment of the industry's woes:

> In 2002 the Dutch company Pharming [Holding] faced severe financial problems and has undergone major restructuring and refinancing. In the U.S., Genzyme Transgenics has cut back on its [clinical] trials [designed to pharm] proteins [from] goat's milk. Much of the work carried out by these companies is further from the market than many might have expected five years ago. The technical barriers have taken longer to hurdle and the costs incurred generally higher than expected. . . . The potential for pharming is enormous but the costs faced in getting the drugs to the market are equally enormous and at the moment as time consuming as traditional methods.[20]

This does not mean that large-scale pharming of cloned animals will never happen. A number of experts predict that, once certain technical problems are overcome and widespread public distrust of cloning declines, the industry will recover and prosper. In fact, some of the companies involved have already managed to regain their footing. In late 2004 the Dutch company Pharming Holding raised huge new funds and plunged forward with an ambitious research and development plan. The success or failure of this company's efforts in the near future may well have a positive or negative effect on the long-term success of the industry in general.

Harvesting Animals' Organs
Animal cloning may also reap medical benefits by creating organs for transplant operations. Such transplants for animals will likely be limited to owners of

Do Transgenic Clones Suffer?

In this excerpt from a 1998 article for the journal *Animals*, economist and animal rights activist Jeremy Rifkin argues that cloning animals is cruel because it can cause animals to suffer undo pain and stress.

Many of the transgenic animal experiments are designed to increase speed of growth, raise weight, and reduce fat. Critics argue that such experiments inevitably lead to increased stress on the animals, more health problems, and unnecessary suffering. Modern animal-husbandry practices bear witness to the cruel toll inflicted on animals in the interest of increasing profits. For example, the modern broiler chicken has been bred to grow to maturity in less than seven weeks and weigh more than five pounds at the time of slaughter. The animal's legs cannot hold its body weight, and as a result, it suffers from painful leg and foot deformities. Now genetic engineers are seeking a patent in the European Patent Office for a transgenic chicken that contains a bovine (cow) hormone gene. The new transgenic chicken is designed to grow to maturity even faster, with leaner meat and earlier sperm production in males virtually assuring more developmental abnormalities, greater stress, more risk of illness, and increased suffering.

expensive racehorses and devoted pet owners who can afford the considerable cost. But the use of these organs for transplants in human patients promises to be much more widespread. Among the animal organs that humans might receive are hearts, kidneys, livers, and bone marrow.

The transplantation of an organ from one species into the body of another species is called a xeno-transplant. It might seem more logical and medically sound to use organs from human donors for such procedures. However, the fact is that there are never enough human donor hearts and other organs to go around. American hospitals estimate that as many as three thousand people in the United States die each year waiting for the donation of an organ for a transplant. Advocates of animal cloning say that cloning might help offer a welcome alternative. They point out that large numbers of animals of various kinds could be created for organ-harvesting purposes.

A question naturally arises: Which animals would be best suited for producing transplant organs for humans? Some experts advocate using monkeys, baboons, and other primates because their genetic makeup is very similar to that of humans. A few transplant operations involving organs from primates (although not cloned ones) have actually been accomplished. In 1984 a baby in California with a heart defect received a heart from a young baboon, for example. And doctors transplanted bone marrow from a baboon into a man infected with the HIV virus in 1995.

Unfortunately for both these patients, their bodies eventually rejected the foreign tissue and they died. Their physicians had anticipated such rejection because the human body always rejects foreign organs, even those from other humans. For this reason, people who have such transplants must take dozens of pills a day to weaken their immune systems and thereby reduce the chances of rejection. Those who take the pills faithfully have about a 75 percent chance of survival.

Not surprisingly, the chance of survival for transplant patients who receive animal organs is even lower. This is because the human body, understandably, perceives tissue from an animal as even more foreign than tissue from a human. In fact, "transplant surgeons [usually] steer away from using animal organs in humans, even though there is a dire shortage of human organs," Gina Kolata points out. "Animals are so genetically different than people. A pig kidney transplanted into a human is just so foreign that the person's immune system will attack it and destroy it."[21]

However, a number of researchers say that this problem can potentially be overcome by genetically modifying animal organs to make them a better match for human bodies. One could extract cells from a pig, for example, and then add proteins from human cells to the pig cells. One could clone these altered cells and create several cloned pigs, each of which would have organs that a human immune system might perceive as human because of the presence of the human proteins. In theory, transplanting these organs into a human might result in only very mild rejection or no rejection at all.

Several companies are now pursuing this goal. Their mission is to create transgenic animals by adding certain human genes to an animal's own genes in hopes that the animal's organs will be far less likely to be rejected by a human body. For the moment, the animal being studied most for transplants is the pig. Most scientists believe there is a higher risk of humans catching diseases from monkeys and other primates than from pigs. This is because primates are for the most part wild animals,

Baby Fae, who received the heart of a baboon in 1984, lived for twenty-one days following the transplant.

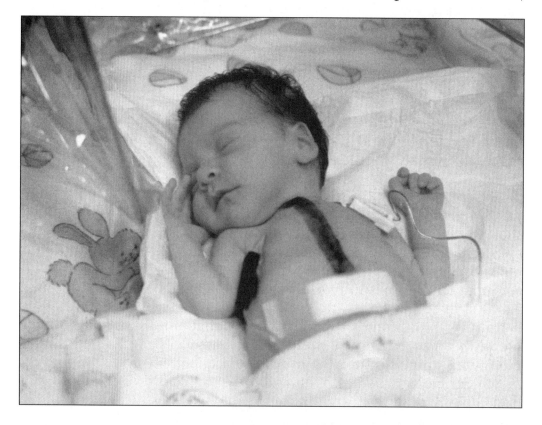

whereas pigs have long been domesticated and under human control. In addition, the size and shape of pigs' organs are very similar to the size and shape of human organs. Some of the leading research in this area has taken place at Advanced Cell Technology in Massachusetts. Researchers there have cloned several pigs, each of which was genetically the same as its siblings. The company has also succeeded in producing transgenic pig clones that have extra human genes.

Creating More Reliable Research Animals

Animal cloning technology also promises to help scientists who conduct research into human diseases and their cures by providing more reliable lab animals. Researchers have long used animals such as mice, rats, rabbits, and guinea pigs to study how various diseases affect living creatures and to test new medicines that might fight those ailments. Supplies of these animals have traditionally come from straightforward breeding programs.

Though knowledge gained from using these animals in experiments is often very valuable, the practice does have certain limitations from a scientific standpoint. For one thing, the lab animals differ from one another physically and mentally, just as humans differ from one another in such ways. By employing the time-consuming, tedious process of selective breeding, lab technicians can produce, say, fifty rats that are all white and about the same size and weight. But these rats are still genetically different. They came from different sets of parents and different litters. And they inevitably possess slightly different habits and reaction times. Thus, a researcher conducting a drug test with these rats cannot be sure whether their reactions are mainly from the effects of the drug or from some unknown genetic differences in the animals themselves.

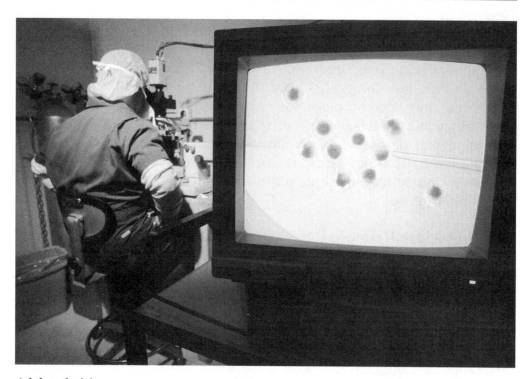

A lab technician injects human DNA into pig's eggs. The hope is to produce animal transplant organs that the human body will not reject.

Lab animals created by cloning rather than traditional breeding would, for all intents and purposes, eliminate 99.9 percent of the differences among lab animals. Also, genetic manipulation techniques could be used on such cloned lab animals. This would theoretically open up new and more efficient avenues for studying diseases. For example, researchers could add to or subtract from an animal's cells the specific genes related to various diseases. In this way, the scientists could create, if they chose to, a mouse with cystic fibrosis. Then they could clone the mouse to produce large numbers of mice with cystic fibrosis, which would allow them to make more reliable studies of the disease.

Although such applications of animal cloning technology are largely still in their infancy, some important advances have been made in recent years. The successful cloning of mice and rats (a process that for various reasons is more difficult than cloning sheep and cows), for example, has opened up many promising avenues in both cloning research and general laboratory research. Some setbacks have occurred. In particular, the high cost of developing herds of sheep to mass-produce drugs has slowed the pace of research in this important area of animal cloning. However, many experts are sure that such setbacks are temporary. They say that the practical ability to clone animals will inevitably revolutionize the fields of biology, medicine, and animal husbandry in the twenty-first century, probably in some ways that no one has yet envisioned.

Chapter 4

Can Cloning Save Endangered Species?

In the mid–twentieth century, scientists pursuing the dream of cloning animals theorized that placing the DNA of a species inside the hollowed-out egg of another species could conceivably produce a living clone. As the years went by and work proceeded toward this goal, some researchers pointed out an amazing potential application for this procedure. Put simply, it might be used to clone the remaining members of a dying species and thereby save that species from extinction.

In addition, a few far-thinking scientists and writers realized that the DNA one implants into the egg does not necessarily have to come from a living animal. The genetic material could theoretically come from a hair cell or other kind of cell preserved from an already dead animal. Therefore, cloning technology seemed to have the potential for resurrecting species that had already gone extinct. The key to success would be making sure that one had the animal's entire genome. Scientists define a genome as all of the genetic material in a given species of plant or animal. (For example, the total DNA that exists in the genes of a dog is a dog's genome.)

Threats to the Planet's Biodiversity

One reason that increasing numbers of researchers considered the idea of using cloning to save endangered species is the alarming rate at which animal species have become either endangered or extinct in the last few centuries. Thousands of species are presently on the endangered list. And experts estimate that as many as a hundred animal and plant species become extinct each day, most of them as a result of pressures created by ever-expanding human civilization.

Some politicians and others who lack the proper training and knowledge have suggested that the loss of a few animal species will not seriously impact the world or humanity. This assessment is shortsighted. Experts warn that over the course of time the unnatural loss of so many species could potentially upset the balance of nature in harmful ways that no one today can predict. In particular, the loss of so many species threatens the integrity of the planet's biodiversity. The

An animal keeper gives medicine to an endangered gorilla. Some researchers see cloning as a possible solution to saving endangered species.

Biodiversity Resource Center at the California Academy of Sciences explains that biodiversity encompasses the following:

> variation in genes enabling organisms to evolve and adapt to new conditions; the number, types, and distribution of species within an ecosystem; and the variety of habitats and communities of different species that interact in a complex web of interdependent relationships.[22]

These natural relationships are very complex, so much so that the loss of one species can affect many other species that coexist in the same ecology (the local physical environment populated by a unique set of plants and animals). The problem is that an increasing number of ecologies are breaking down or at least are under mounting stress. And humans are often part of or connected to these ecologies. "Human survival itself may depend upon reversing this accelerating threat to species diversity," the Biodiversity Resource Center points out.

> Among the millions of undescribed species [those species that humans have not yet studied and that might disappear before they are studied] are important new sources of food, medicine, and other products. When a species vanishes, we lose access to the survival strategies encoded in its genes through millions of years of evolution. We lose the opportunity to understand those strategies which may hold absolutely essential options for our own survival as a species. . . . Many indigenous human cultures have also been driven to extinction by the same forces that have destroyed and continue to threaten non-human species. It is estimated that since 1900, more than 90 tribes of aboriginal peoples have become extinct in the Amazon [River] Basin.[23]

Humans are Accelerating the Rate of Animal Extinctions

Over the course of the past 500 million years, many millions of animal species that once roamed Earth or swam in the seas went extinct for one reason or another. Some of these reasons are explainable. The dinosaurs and numerous other species, for example, appear to have been wiped out by the catastrophic effects of the giant impact of a comet or asteroid 65 million years ago. Other species die from more gradual causes, such as the inability to adapt to climatic and other changes in the environment. One thing all of these extinctions have in common is that they were natural and therefore beyond the bounds of human control.

By contrast, human beings themselves have caused numerous species to become extinct out of thoughtlessness, lack of foresight, apathy, or sheer greed. Overhunting various animals for their meat, hides, or horns; cutting down forests to clear the way for cities and roads; and poisoning the environment with toxic substances are among the major human causes of animal extinction. The rate of animal extinctions caused by humans is rapidly accelerating. A growing number of scientists believe that cloning may help alleviate this problem.

The Case of the Enderby Cow

Even before the successful cloning of Dolly the sheep, Gene the bull, and other animals, scientists realized that cloning might one day help maintain Earth's rich biodiversity. In theory, it seemed that an endangered species could be saved, even if the DNA donor was the very last of its kind. Such theory, which even a few scientists viewed as a flight of fancy as late as the early 1990s, suddenly became reality later in the same decade. A mere two years after Dolly's birth, cloning technology saved its first animal from the brink of extinction.

That fortunate creature was the Enderby cow, a rare breed of cow native to New Zealand. In the mid–nineteenth century, several cattle ranchers tried to start a ranch on Enderby, a small, barren island off the coast of mainland New Zealand. After only a few years, the ranchers abandoned the project and left. The cattle remained, however. And over the course of

This calf was the first to be born naturally from one of the clones of Lady, the last surviving Enderby cow.

the century and a half that followed, their descendants adapted to the island's harsh conditions, undergoing distinct physical changes in the process. By 1992, one result of this evolution was a new breed of cattle.

But there was a problem. A large population of Enderby cattle had developed in the wild. Local authorities worried that the beasts might eat too many local plants and ruin the island's fragile ecology. New Zealand federal authorities agreed and ordered the herd destroyed as a safety measure.

Before the mass slaughter began, however, some New Zealand scientists vehemently argued that it would be wrong to eradicate an entire species. They urged the government to allow a single Enderby cow to live, at least so that it might be studied. Agricultural officials agreed and shipped the cow, which they named Lady, to a scientific lab on New Zealand's mainland.

For a while it seemed as though Lady would live out the rest of her days in obscurity in that lab. But when Ian Wilmut's team cloned Dolly in 1996, the New Zealand researchers realized that it might be possible to clone cells taken from Lady and thereby save her species. Using a procedure similar to the one that produced Dolly, they took some cells from Lady's ovaries and grew them into embryos. They then implanted the embryos into the wombs of some cows of a different breed, which acted as surrogate mothers. The first calf was born in July 1998. By 2002, cloning had produced five Enderby cows, the nucleus of a new herd. Several calves were born to these animals in 2003 and 2004, further expanding the herd.

Cell Banks for Cloning Endangered Species

The last-minute rescue of the Enderby cow species demonstrated to the world that cloning is indeed a viable method of saving endangered animals. Inspired and encouraged by the achievement, biologists, zoologists, and other scientists around the world pushed forward with ambitious plans to save other species. Among these efforts was an attempt to use cloning technology to save the giant panda.

A bearlike creature with beautiful black and yellowish-white markings, an adult panda can weigh as much as 330 pounds or more. The giant panda is native to central China, where it usually dwells in cool, damp bamboo forests at elevations of five thousand to thirteen thousand feet. In fact, bamboo constitutes the main staple of its diet (although it will occasionally eat other plants or, if it is hungry enough, small animals). Because the bamboo forests are rapidly disappearing, thanks to encroaching human settlement, populations of giant pandas are dwindling. Only a thousand, and perhaps fewer, remain in the wild.

Chinese scientists became determined to not allow the giant panda to disappear forever. They instituted a crash program in 1998 and only a year later succeeded in cloning a panda embryo from adult panda cells. This was considered a remarkable achievement because, for various technical reasons, bear cells have proven unusually difficult to clone successfully. It is not surprising, therefore, that so far all attempts to produce a live cloned giant panda have failed. However, Chinese researchers are still trying and are confident they will eventually succeed. Late in 2004 they announced they had taken another step toward their goal by creating a giant panda cell bank, which will ensure them an ample supply of the rare genetic material required for their program.

Meanwhile, similar advances occurred at the San Diego Zoo, one of the world's leading sanctuaries of endangered animals. Back in 1975, the institution's chief biologist, Kurt Benirschke, had begun freezing cells from endangered species. At the time the program had nothing to do with cloning. Rather, its purpose was to preserve the cells so that their genetic material could be studied and compared to that of various similar species.

After the announcement of Dolly's existence, however, Benirschke realized that the cells he had been collecting might also be used to bring some endangered species back from the brink. "The possibili-

Chinese scientists have made major strides in recent years in their efforts to use cloning to save the giant panda.

ties for zoos are enormous," he stated. "I would love to excite the international community to save as many cells as they can from as many animals as possible."[24] Translating this call into action, other institutions and labs around the world are currently creating similar cell banks to preserve animal DNA.

Increasing Genetic Diversity

Benirschke and his colleagues also say that saving species from ex-

A San Diego Zoo researcher holds a refrigerated mammal cell. The zoo has a large collection of cells from endangered species.

tinction constitutes only one biological and ecological benefit of advancing animal cloning technology. They point out that the technology could conceivably be used to increase the genetic diversity of a dwindling species. At first glance, this idea seems to contradict one of the more popular public perceptions about cloning—that it creates only genetically identical copies of individual plants or animals. One might wonder how making copies, each with the same genome, can increase genetic diversity.

In reality, however, cloning, aided by animal cell banks like the one in San Diego, might be used to expand diversity by replacing genes that have been lost from an animal's genome. Consider those species that have dwindled to the point where only a few individuals survive, such as the Spanish ibex and South China tiger. When millions of these animals existed, there was considerable variation and diversity within the genome of each species. But with only a few animals left, that diversity is limited. However, cells stored at the San Diego Zoo or elsewhere could theoretically be cloned to produce new individuals of such a species. Researchers would bring these new animals together with the remaining ones in the wild and the two groups would interbreed, a process that would reintroduce lost genes, adding diversity to the genome of the species.

Experts admit that such experiments involving the last members of a dying species will not be easy and must be handled carefully and delicately. For one thing, the egg cells for the cloning process must be removed from the few remaining individuals in the wild. And there is a danger that the act of removing these cells may harm these rare and sometimes fragile creatures. Also, suitable surrogate mothers must be found to carry the embryos created during the cloning process. As Benirschke and other experts point out, science has the advantage that transfers of embryos from one subspecies to another have already been accomplished. Angus cows carried the first cloned Enderby calves, for example. And researchers from Ithaca, New York, and Suffolk, England, have succeeded in growing a zebra in the womb of a horse.

Various members of the large group of cat subspecies have also proven to be useful as egg suppliers and as surrogates for carrying cat clones. In 2003 a team of scientists at the Audubon Center for Research of Endangered Species, in New Orleans, succeeded in cloning a rare and endangered cat species—the African wildcat. The researchers took DNA from one of the few remaining wildcats and injected it into the hollowed-out egg of a domestic cat. A few months later a cloned wildcat was born. Six others soon followed, for a total of two males and five females. The New Orleans team hopes to clone two other endangered cat species—the black-footed cat (native to southern Africa) and the rusty spotted cat (from India and Sri Lanka)—by the end of 2005.

Cloning the Family Pet

Though important, these recent developments in cloning wildcats did not garner nearly as much attention as the announcement that a domesticated cat—someone's pet—had been successfully cloned. Scientists had long known that cloning beloved pets was possible in theory. But most did not involve themselves in this area, partly because people's emotional attachment to their pets makes the work highly controversial.

However, some people have demonstrated that they are willing to pay a great deal of money to clone their pets. In 1998, for instance, an American millionaire offered some researchers $5 million to try to clone his dog. Though this effort failed, the big commercial potential of cloning pets inspired several companies to launch research and development in this area of cloning.

At the Audubon Institute Center for Research of Endangered Species, an American shorthair cat gave birth to an African wildcat kitten grown from a frozen embryo.

The most successful of these companies so far has been Genetic Savings and Clone, based in Sausalito, California, which announced its successful cloning of a domestic house cat in December 2004. (Actually, this was the company's first "made-to-order" house cat; it had first cloned a domesticated cat for experimental purposes in December 2001.) The made-to-order cat, named Little Nicky, was cloned for a Texas woman whose seventeen-year-old pet, Nicky, had died in 2003. The woman paid $50,000 and claims to be extremely happy with the results. Genetic Savings and Clone describes its cat-cloning process this way:

In December 2004, technicians from Genetic Savings and Clone present a Texas woman with her made-to-order cloned cat, Little Nicky.

> The cloning process begins with gene banking, in which a veterinarian takes a small tissue biopsy from the animal to be cloned, also

known as the genetic donor. The tissue biopsy is transported . . . to our PetBank. The tissue is cultured (grown) at our PetBank. The cells are then [preserved] in liquid nitrogen, where they can be stored indefinitely. An egg from the same species being cloned . . . [has its] genetic material removed. The egg is then ready to receive the genes of the genetic donor. . . . The treated donor cell is combined with the . . . egg by electrofusion [use of an electric charge], resulting in a single-celled cloned embryo, ready for transfer into a surrogate mother. To become a surrogate mother, an animal must be in heat, or estrus. When the surrogate goes into estrus, we insert cloned embryos into her oviduct, resulting in pregnancy. The surrogate carries the embryos to term . . . and gives birth to kittens who are clones of the genetic donor.[25]

The company is employing a similar process in experiments with dogs and claims it will be able to produce made-for-order dogs by the end of 2005.

Some people have raised objections or at least pointed out inherent drawbacks to such pet cloning. First, they say, a person who pays for this service should understand that the beloved pet is not actually being brought back to life. Though the cloned animal looks just like the original one, it does not have the same memories, intelligence level, disposition, and so forth. It is a new animal whose brain is essentially a blank slate. Also, cloning is an extremely expensive process and is likely to remain so for a long time. Most pet owners will not be able to afford it, so it may come to be seen as an extravagant and elitist luxury of the rich.

Bringing Back Extinct Species?

Thanks to companies like Genetic Savings and Clone, resurrecting an animal that has been dead for a few weeks or months has proven to be doable, if re-pugnant to some people. Can the same technology be used to bring back a creature that died ten years ago? How about a hundred years ago? Or a thousand? Or tens of millions? If so, could dinosaurs be cloned so that they would walk the Earth again? As many people know, this is the basic premise of Michael Crichton's hugely popular novel *Jurassic Park* and Steven Spielberg's equally popular series of films based on it.

A number of scientists say that, strictly in theory, the science behind the book and films is basically correct. If one had some usable dinosaur DNA, he or she might be able to clone a dinosaur. However, several technical difficulties separate the theory from reality. Perhaps the chief obstacle scientists must overcome is that there are no living dinosaurs from which to take cells and DNA for the cloning procedure. So the DNA would have to be found lingering somewhere in the natural world.

But where in nature would one look to find dinosaur DNA? Contrary to popular belief, the fossilized remains of dinosaurs do not contain such genetic material. Over time, nature very efficiently recycles the remains of dead creatures. Tissues, bones, and so forth decay and are transformed into soil, plants, and other animals, which themselves die, decompose, and recycle over the eons. In fact, it is likely that each and every person alive on Earth today has at least a few atoms in his or her body that were once part of the body of a dinosaur. (However, these are a few individual, widely scattered atoms, not complex, highly organized DNA molecules, each containing thousands of atoms.) Thus, all of the dinosaur genomes exposed to soil, water, and weather have long since disintegrated.

What about dinosaur genomes that were somehow shielded from the ravages of erosion? This is the way Crichton got around this problem in his story.

In Steven Spielberg's first Jurassic Park *film, scientists examine a dinosaur egg created through the cloning process.*

He had some scientists find dinosaur DNA in dinosaur blood found in the stomachs of insects that had bitten dinosaurs. The insects had been trapped in amber (solidified tree sap) and thereby perfectly preserved for millions of years. Crichton did not simply invent this idea out of thin air. He based it on the fact that scientists have indeed found the DNA of insects and plants some 30 million years old preserved in amber.

Problems with Ancient DNA

However, this DNA is not from dinosaurs. Moreover, the insect DNA found in amber contains only tiny fragments of the original genetic material. The same would be true of any dinosaur DNA that might be found in a piece of amber. It is highly unlikely that the complete sequence of DNA in a dinosaur's genome will have survived intact. There may be thousands or even millions of pieces missing, so it may well be impossible to put it back together. And this will definitely be a major obstacle to cloning extremely ancient creatures like dinosaurs. As scientists Rob DeSalle and David Lindley explain:

> Even if someone has managed to isolate a whole stack of little fragments of what [he or she] thinks is dinosaur DNA . . . [the] trouble is, you don't know what the genome looks like in the first place, so it's going to be difficult to figure out how to put these pieces together in the right order. . . . But apart from all of this, the real problem is in assuming that you have all the pieces of a dinosaur genome in the first place. Even though bits of DNA a few hundred bases [individual genes] long can quite plausibly survive, you are going to need millions of such pieces to make a whole genome. Judging from what's been extracted from 30-million-year-old insects, you'll be lucky to retrieve just a few small fragments. The chances that the entire genome is still there, even in tiny pieces, seem remote.[26]

Scientists who dream of resurrecting dinosaurs face other problems as well. For instance, even if dinosaur DNA could be found and even if that DNA was chemically complete and sound, there would be no guarantee that cloning that DNA would produce a dinosaur. The modern animal egg used to incubate the DNA and grow an embryo may not be able to "read" the genetic instructions of a beast that is both ancient and extinct. "You can't just throw DNA from one creature into the egg of another and expect something to start growing," DeSalle and Lindley point out.

> Different eggs know different things [about DNA codes], and to make a dinosaur from your dinosaur genome, you need to have an egg that's

Complexity Is an Obstacle to Cloning Extinct Species

In this excerpt from their book *The Science of Jurassic Park and the Lost World*, Rob DeSalle, of the American Museum of Natural History, and David Lindley, former editor of *Science* magazine, offer an intriguing analogy to demonstrate the tremendous complexity of genetic material, which is a major obstacle to using cloning to resurrect extinct species.

If you took one of your own chromosomes and magnified it until it was the width of a very skinny rubber band, it would be about 10 miles long. So imagine two people holding the ends of a 10-mile-long rubber band and twisting and twisting and twisting, until the whole thing is raveled into a ball the size of your fist. And now think about trying to figure out precisely the way it's arranged and how you would describe that configuration to someone else, so that another rubber band could be twisted up in exactly the same way. Complicated, isn't it? . . . Although there's a good deal of broad similarity in the packaging of DNA in quite widely varying species, the fine details of chromosome structure are decidedly not all the same. And those details may have something to do with what makes a human a human and a chimp a chimp.

set up to do the same things a dinosaur egg needs to do. . . . The huge variety of cells in a body all grow from a single egg cell—and just how that happens no one really knows. We do not know that the instructions for making all those cell types reside ultimately [and exclusively] in the DNA. It's therefore clear that the egg cell has to come equipped with complex [chemical] mechanisms that can read and translate those instructions correctly. . . . To grow dinosaurs from the dinosaur genome, you're going to need [a great deal of] guesswork and a lot of luck.[27]

Thus, unless some presently unknown way to recover intact dinosaur DNA is discovered, cloning dinosaurs and other very ancient beasts is likely to remain strictly in the realm of entertaining science fiction.

Chapter 5

The Controversial Advent of Human Cloning

When news of the cloned sheep Dolly's birth echoed around the world in 1997, many scientists immediately began diligent efforts to clone animals for research purposes, commercial markets, and saving endangered species. Although important and controversial in and of themselves, these efforts took a decided backseat to what most people perceived as a much larger issue: the viability of cloning human beings. If a complex mammal like a sheep could be cloned, the general reasoning went, science could not be all that far away from applying the same kind of technology to people.

A number of scientists certainly agreed with this conclusion. In their view, human cloning had suddenly become not only possible but also quite probable. And some researchers got right to work. Progress in these labs was rapid at first. The first major step—cloning a human embryo—occurred in December 1998 when a team of scientists in a lab in Seoul, South Korea, succeeded in creating such an embryo consisting of a few cells. Various other labs around the world soon repeated this experiment.

The next steps in the process of human cloning seemed clear enough: to create larger and certifiably healthy embryos; to implant them in human wombs; and to grow them safely to term. However, these steps were not taken. (At least that is the consensus of most reputable scientists; a few researchers widely seen as less reputable claim to have cloned human infants but have not provided any proof.) For reasons that are still uncertain, the Korean scientists destroyed the embryos they had created. And over time increasing numbers of scientists became reluctant to proceed with human cloning projects. Indeed, progress in human cloning has slowed significantly in the past few years as labs and researchers who once contemplated it have redirected their time and resources to other areas of research.

This researcher at Seoul National University is creating a cloned embryo. The South Koreans have made pioneering strides in human cloning.

The main reason for this remarkable turn of events has been fear of adverse public and governmental reactions to such work. The fact is that, since the moment

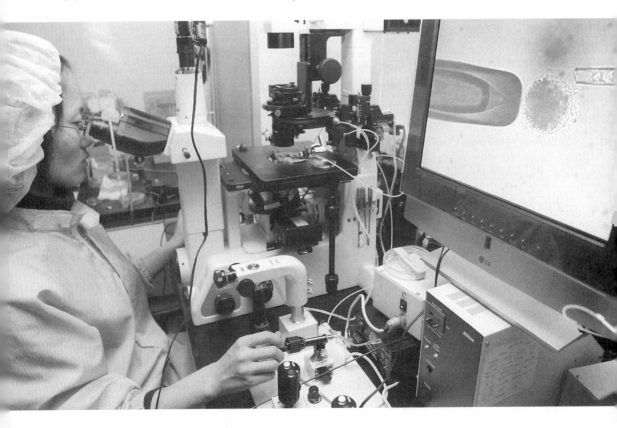

the Roslin Institute announced Dolly's existence, a fierce public debate has raged over whether cloning people is ethical and moral. The degree to which this debate will affect progress in human cloning technology in both the short and long terms is for the moment too difficult to predict with any certainty.

Ethical Debates Discourage Human Cloning

The ethical debate about human cloning has several dimensions. But at its heart for most people are what are best termed as religious or spiritual concerns. The perception among many devout members of most major religions is that creating humans through the artificial process of cloning will somehow interfere with God's plan or wishes. Shortly after the announcement of Dolly's birth, for example, Pope John Paul II condemned the very idea of human cloning, calling it a tragic attempt by humans to imitate God's unique and special life-giving powers.

The pope spoke only for Catholics, of course. However, large numbers of Protestants, Muslims, and Jews agreed with the basic points of his argument. In March 1997 *Time* magazine polled a random sample of Americans about the issue of human cloning. A hefty 74 percent said they viewed cloning humans as being against the will of God. Later in that same year a report by the National Bioethics Advisory Commission (a group that advises the U.S. president on the ethical uses of science) reached a similar conclusion. "Human beings should not probe the fundamental secrets or mysteries of life, which belong to God," the commission stated.

Human beings lack the [divine] authority to make certain decisions about the beginning or ending of life. . . . Human beings are fallible [whereas God is infallible]. . . . Human beings do not have the knowledge . . . [or] the power to control the outcomes of actions or processes

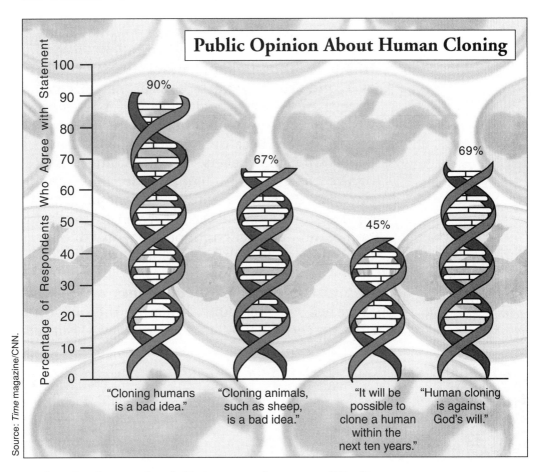

Public Opinion About Human Cloning

Source: *Time* magazine/CNN.

Percentage of Respondents Who Agree with Statement

90%

"Cloning humans is a bad idea."

67%

"Cloning animals, such as sheep, is a bad idea."

45%

"It will be possible to clone a human within the next ten years."

69%

"Human cloning is against God's will."

that is the mark of divine omnipotence [God's almighty power].[28]

Those who supported research into human cloning responded with the argument that people of different faiths have different views of where humanity's domain ends and God's domain begins. And in a society like that of the United States, which has laws protecting religious freedom, no single religious group or view should be forced on everyone. Moreover, advocates of cloning said, failing to develop the new technology might end up hurting society by denying it many potential benefits. A progressive New York–based think tank summed up this view, asking:

Do advocates of supernatural or spiritual agendas have truly meaningful qualifications to contribute to [the human cloning] debate? Surely everyone has the right to be heard. But we believe there is a very real danger that research with enormous potential benefits may be suppressed solely because it conflicts with some people's religious beliefs. It is important to recognize that similar religious objections were once raised against autopsies, anesthesia, artificial insemination, and the entire genetic revolution of our day—yet enormous benefits have accrued from each of these developments.[29]

Protesters outside a Massachusetts biotech firm make their position known by equating human cloning with Nazism and death.

Dubious Claims of Cloned Infants

As revealed by later polls similar to the one conducted by *Time* in 1997, this second view—that hu-

man cloning technology should go forward—is presently held by only a small minority of citizens in most countries. As a result, a majority of leading genetics labs are not pursuing human cloning. In addition to the fear of becoming the central focus of an ethical controversy, researchers at these labs have trouble raising the necessary funds. This is because the controversy has also caused many financial backers to use their money in other ways. Even the Roslin Institute found several of its backers withdrawing support between 2001 and 2004.

Under these conditions, most of the labs that are presently trying to clone human babies are run by fringe groups with little or no credibility in the scientific community. By far the most famous of these groups is the one that calls itself the Raelians. In the 1990s, this Canadian organization set up a genetics lab and corporation called Clonaid that was for a while widely advertised as the front-runner in the race to create the first cloned human. Margaret Talbot, of the New America Foundation (a think tank that promotes open debate of controversial issues), describes the Raelians and their belief system, of which cloning is a central tenet:

> Since 1974, they have raised $7 million toward the construction of an "embassy" where alien visitors could be welcomed to our planet in style. Their followers, who hold fast to the ideal of everlasting life created through technology, are a devoted lot. Their leader . . . Raël, a French-born former race-car driver . . . says [that] he had an encounter with a four-foot-tall alien . . . whose flying saucer had landed atop a volcano in southern France. From this creature, he heard the message that humans had been created [through cloning] in a laboratory by advanced beings from another planet who had mastered genetics and cell biology.[30]

Led by Brigitte Boisselier, a French chemist, the Clonaid team pushed forward with human cloning research. In December 2002 spokesmen for the team claimed they had succeeded in cloning a baby girl, symbolically named Eve. Clonaid later said it had cloned four more infants and that several more women were pregnant with cloned children and would soon give birth. Mainstream scientists naturally demanded proof for such fantastic claims. Boisselier at first promised that genetic testing and other proof would be forthcoming, but she and her associates quickly reneged on their promise. They said they were afraid that revealing Eve's true identity might aid U.S. courts that wanted to try to take her away from her rightful parents.

Another news-making human cloning team is headed by Panayiotis Zavos, of the Kentucky Center for Reproductive Medicine, and Italian scientist Severino Antinori. Their cloning efforts are proceeding at an undisclosed location outside of the United States. Like the Raelians, Zavos and Antinori have been generally discredited or at least discounted by the vast majority of scientists.

Resurrecting Deceased Loved Ones

A few mainstream scientists continue to talk about human cloning, however. And occasional strides have been made in labs deemed legitimate by the scientific community. The most outstanding example so far occurred in February 2004 when another South Korean team, this one led by Dr. Hwang Woo-suk, announced the successful cloning of several large, well-developed, and apparently healthy human embryos. (These embryos are much more viable for cloning people than the ones created in Korea in 1998.)

Dr. Hwang and other scientists involved in this work admit that the subject is controversial and that cloning people is a concept that will never appeal to

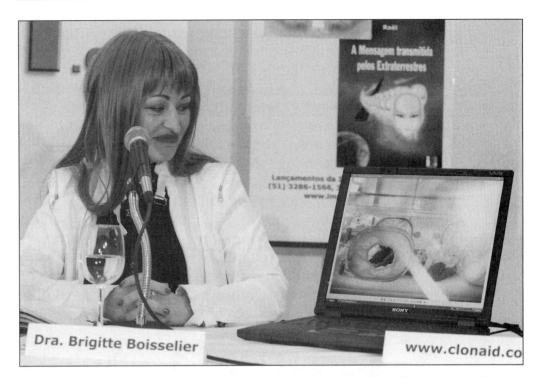

Dra. Brigitte Boisselier   www.clonaid.co

Brigitte Boisselier, head of the Clonaid cloning project, displays a photo of the third human infant she claims to have cloned.

everyone. However, they say, human cloning has many potential benefits for both individuals and society as a whole. And they are confident that in time many people who are now suspicious of the technology will come to feel that the benefits outweigh the drawbacks.

Some of the benefits they cite are quite similar to those touted for cloning animals. Just as some people would seriously consider bringing back a beloved pet, some find the idea of bringing back deceased human loved ones appealing. In fact, a number of individuals have already expressed the desire to have lost husbands, wives, children, or other relatives cloned. In 2000, for example, an unnamed American couple approached some scientists about the possibility of cloning their son, who had died at the age of ten months. The parents were both fertile and could have had another child the natural way. However, as noted journalist Margaret Talbot, who made the story public, emphasizes:

They did not want another child. They wanted *this* child. And before long they began to believe that the longing they felt was telling them something quite specific—that their dead baby's genes were crying out, as a ghost might, to express themselves again in this world. The idea preoccupied them that their little son's genotype [genome] deserved another chance, that it had disappeared by mistake and could be brought back by intention.[31]

The parents in question are not alone. Each year the number of people who express the desire to clone deceased loved ones grows larger. The Web Site of the Human Cloning Foundation (in Atlanta, Georgia), a group that promotes the concept of hu-

Clonaid Responds to Its Critics

In 2004 Dr. Brigitte Boisselier, leader of Clonaid's efforts to clone humans, defended those efforts in this statement (published on Clonaid's Web site), aimed at United Nations officials who had been critical of the Clonaid program.

Centuries ago, twins were killed because primitive people thought they were evil. Today ethicists are telling you the same about cloned children. Will you let them decide for you? Reproductive cloning is giving life to a few individuals and cannot harm any one. The Hollywood stories of monstrous defects have no real scientific bases if you listen to real experts and I would be happy to demonstrate this to you. In the future, reproductive cloning will enable all of us to live eternally. This is what His Holiness Rael, founder of the Raelian Movement and of Clonaid, announced 30 years ago. . . . By declaring human cloning a crime against humanity, you will just slow down an unescapable process, as sooner or later, not only will we beat most of the diseases thanks to stem cells but we will also beat death thanks to cloning and a majority of people on this planet will request it. The real crime against Humanity is to deny the right to . . . explore science freely and its wonderful benefits. I will be available any time to explain more about what Clonaid has achieved as I believe it is a major step for humanity.

man cloning, receives thousands of messages a year from people wanting to clone dead relatives. One was from a man who identified himself simply as Thomas. "I lost my only son in a very bad and unfortunate . . . [car] accident last year," he stated.

> He was 11 years old . . . and he was my only [child]. My new wife cannot have children and my ex-wife misses our son very much. Everyone knows that the cloned child would not be the child we lost but he would be similar and people that can't have another child from their own blood line are very depressed people. . . . I really feel sad that people are so against all the great benefits this new technology could bring to the human race. God gave us the freedom to reproduce and create life. . . . God and God alone sent us the people that have discovered these new technologies. God expects us to use this new technology to our benefit.[32]

In his letter, "Thomas" brought up an important aspect of cloning deceased humans, for whatever reason it might be done. Namely, cloning a person will duplicate only his or her physical appearance and other genetic elements, not the person's personality and memories. Thus, the cloned person will grow up with its own personality, experiences, likes and dislikes, and personal desires and goals. Officials at the Human Cloning Foundation and others who counsel people about cloning deceased loved ones are always careful to make sure that those involved are aware of this crucial fact.

Hope for Infertile Couples?
The Human Cloning Foundation and other similar groups also receive many requests from infertile couples who want to clone a child rather than adopt one. Some people see this as one of the major ways

cloning will improve people's lives, mainly by providing them with additional reproductive choices. According to human cloning advocate J.P. Lovell:

> Cloning technology offers infertile couples the promise of greatly improving the odds of having a baby. An infertile man can have sperm cloned and the undamaged sperm used. Likewise, an infertile woman can have an egg cloned and the fertile egg used for conception. . . . Regardless of ethical debates about human cloning . . . it must be a choice offered to infertile parents. Like a truly democratic nation such as ours, this choice must be protected and upheld.[33]

Other people disagree and say that for ethical reasons infertile couples should avoid cloning and stick to traditional, accepted methods of nonsexual reproduction.

What are these accepted methods, and how might cloning offer an alternative to them? First, there is in vitro fertilization, in which a woman's egg and a man's sperm are joined in the lab instead of in her womb. But doctors point out that this method does not work for everyone. A second technique is used in cases in which a woman's eggs or man's sperm are defective or nonexistent. If the man is infertile, for example, the couple can accept sperm donated by another man, which combines with the woman's egg to produce a child. The drawback of this method is that the baby will carry the genes of only one of the parents.

In theory, cloning could get around some of these difficulties. In the case of an infertile man, for instance, his genetic material could be extracted from some of his cells and transplanted into his mate's egg. Some researchers say that cloning might also be a way for gay couples and people with genetic disorders to have children.

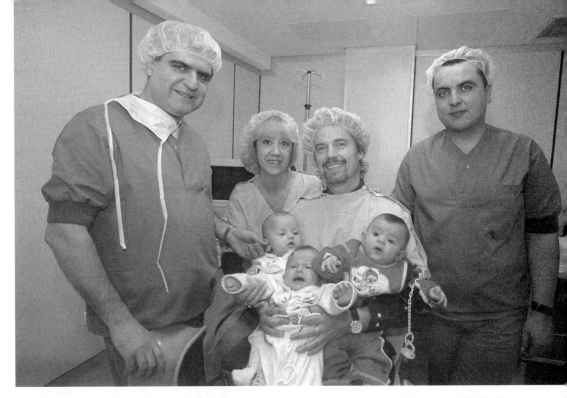

Advances in Stem Cell Research

Another benefit often cited for human cloning technology does not involve creating completely new human beings. Again mirroring research in the area of animal cloning, some medical experts believe that human cloning techniques will make it easier to create replacement organs and tissues for sick or injured people. Although using cloning to produce animal organs for human transplants certainly shows promise, that technique still has the problem of rejection by the immune system. So using animal organs in humans will ultimately fail in a certain percentage of patients. In contrast, if the patient's *own* cells are used to grow the organs or tissues, the match will be genetically perfect and no rejection would occur.

The concept of growing human organs and tissues by cloning builds on existing knowledge and techniques in another controversial area of medical research—stem cells. Stem cells are undifferentiated, or unspecialized, cells—that is, cells that have not yet received specific instructions to become heart, liver, bone, or other sorts of cells. In the 1980s some researchers managed to stop the normal development

These three Turkish babies were born from an egg fertilized by sperm grown in a lab from stem cells.

Animal Cloners and Human Cloners at Odds?

Dr. Panayiotis Zavos, one of the scientists who is presently conducting active experiments in human cloning, claims that scientists involved in animal cloning have not been supportive of his program. He aired his view on the matter in an open letter in a Scottish newspaper (the *Sunday Herald*, October 21, 2001), excerpted here.

Since our announcement . . . that we intend to use reproductive cloning as a means to help infertile couples, we have received nothing but opposition from those in the animal cloning field. Because of the limited knowledge of these procedures in the scientific community, we have organized, hosted and attended meetings to discuss and debate the issues of human reproductive cloning. These have involved scientists from all over the world. However, the "animal cloners" feel they have exhausted all possible technologies and have come to the conclusion that the technology is not safe to use in humans, and would like the world to believe this notion. Let's examine the facts. Firstly, the poor cloning success rates noted by these animal cloners are mainly due to experiments that were poorly designed, poorly executed, and poorly understood and interpreted. . . . Also, when the animals died, the cause of death was unclear. . . . Animal cloning and its difficulties appear to be species-specific, and the data cannot be extrapolated with a great degree of accuracy to the human species.

Dr. Panayiotis Zavos claims that animal-cloners have openly opposed his research.

process at the embryonic level. The cells of the embryo continued to divide and grow, but only into more undifferentiated embryonic cells. These special cells came to be called embryonic stem cells.

A number of scientists have proposed that embryonic stem cells could be cloned and grown into a mass of undifferentiated tissue of any size that is needed. In theory, researchers could use various methods to convert this unspecialized mass into any kind of tissue desired. That tissue could then be used to replace or repair an injured or diseased organ.

However promising embryonic stem cells may be, some people continue to voice ethical concerns about their use. The chief concern is that human embryos are both created and destroyed in the cloning process. In recent years some scientists have been investigating what might be an alternative that does not utilize embryonic cells. Instead, it employs so-called adult stem cells. These are undifferentiated cells found in several of the body's organs. It is believed that the natural purpose of these cells (which exist in far smaller numbers than differentiated cells in these organs) is to aid in tissue regeneration after an injury. Physician and noted futurist Dr. Patrick Dixon explains how adult stem cell technology might benefit people:

> Suppose you have a heart attack. [A] surgeon talks to you about using your own stem cells in an experimental treatment. You agree. A sample of bone marrow is taken from your hips, and processed [grown in culture] using standard equipment found in most oncology centers for treating leukemia. The result is a concentrated number of special bone marrow cells, which are then injected back into your own body, either into a vein in your arm, or perhaps direct into the heart itself. The surgeon is returning your own unaltered stem cells back to you, to whom these cells legally belong. . . . Your own adult stem cells are available right now. No factory is involved, nor any pharmaceutical company sales team. What is more, there [is] no . . . risk of tissue rejection, no risk of cancer.[34]

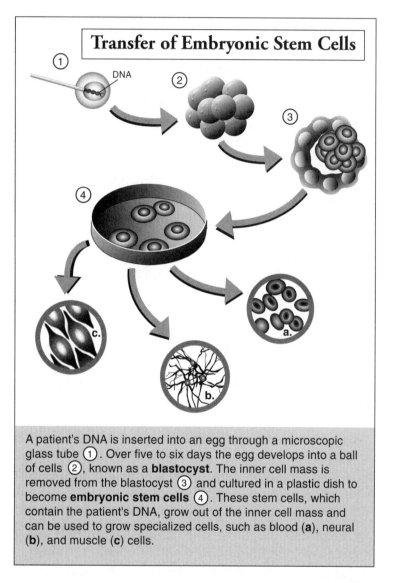

Transfer of Embryonic Stem Cells

A patient's DNA is inserted into an egg through a microscopic glass tube ①. Over five to six days the egg develops into a ball of cells ②, known as a **blastocyst**. The inner cell mass is removed from the blastocyst ③ and cultured in a plastic dish to become **embryonic stem cells** ④. These stem cells, which contain the patient's DNA, grow out of the inner cell mass and can be used to grow specialized cells, such as blood (**a**), neural (**b**), and muscle (**c**) cells.

Dixon and other researchers say that many other kinds of transplants involving both cloned embryonic stem cells and cultured adult stem cells will be possible, creating a veritable medical revolution. Burn victims might receive healthy new skin grown from their own tissues; people with spinal cord injuries might have their spines repaired; and hearts, lungs, kidneys, bladders, and other organs might be made to order for specific patients, saving or extending their lives. In addition, stem cell technology might significantly enhance plastic, reconstructive, and cosmetic surgery.

Dixon also makes the point that advances in stem cells, including both the cloned embryonic kind and the adult kind, are presently proceeding at an accelerated rate. "Over 2,000 new research papers on embryonic or adult stem cells are published in reputable scientific journals every year," he says.

> Stem cell technology is developing so fast that many stem cell scientists are unaware of important progress by others in their own or closely related fields. They are unable to keep up. The most interesting work is often unpublished, or waiting to be published. There is also of course commercial and reputational rivalry, which can on occasion tempt scientists to downplay the significance of other people's results (or their claims).[35]

Is Human Cloning Inevitable?

The arguments over which kind of stem cell is ethically right to use mirror the larger debates over the morality of human cloning itself. Such differences of opinion are likely to continue for a long time to come. However, no one can argue with the plain fact that the proverbial genie has been released from the bottle. Several scientists, bioethicists, and politicians point out that, whether for good or ill, it is now too late to stop human cloning from happening sooner or later. The basic technology exists, they say. So it is only a matter of time before someone carries the potential of that technology to its limits.

In fact, it could be that humans will one day clone themselves in large degree because they are compelled to do so. In a thought-provoking essay written in the late 1990s, noted chemical engineer Rudy Baum suggested that human cloning is inevitable because humans are inevitably driven to learn and

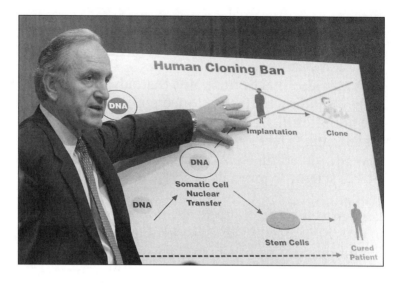

Senator Tom Harkin of Iowa uses a chart in a speech given in the Senate in 2001. Harkin argued that stem cell research holds great potential to eradicate disease.

progress and in the process to transform and reshape nature. The "moral Rubicon," or point of no return, "has already been crossed," he said.

> Is that a moral catastrophe for humans? No. Is it the mark of our ultimate hubris [arrogance], our need to "play God"? Certainly. Playing God is what humans do for a living. We've been doing it for centuries. We rearranged the natural landscape through plant and animal breeding. We discovered vaccination and antibiotics to defeat plagues that once decimated populations. We exterminated species because they were in our way. We created reproductive technologies to aid people who would otherwise not be able to have children. . . . Now we've learned how to clone animals and, probably, people. It's all part of a . . . technological imperative that is as unstoppable as the passage of time.[36]

If this is indeed the case, humanity's only rational course may be to find some way of strictly regulating, and thereby controlling, this powerful and controversial technology.

Notes

Introduction: A New and Controversial Technology

1. Lee M. Silver, *Remaking Eden: Cloning and Beyond in a Brave New World.* New York: Avon, 1997, p. 12.
2. "Statement of Senator Edward M. Kennedy," Hearing on Cloning, *Congressional Record*, March 5, 2002.
3. Silver, *Remaking Eden*, p. 2.

Chapter 1: Plant Cloning: From Nature to Agriculture

4. Bijal P. Trivedi, "Grasshoppers Used to Fight 'Worst Water Weed,'" *National Geographic*, April 1, 2003. http://news.nationalgeographic.com/news/2003/04/0401_030401_tv hyacinth.html.
5. Phytocultures Ltd., "Other Plants: An Overview," 2004. www.phytocultures.com/other_overview.asp.
6. Larissa Parsley, "Transgenic Plants: A Budding Controversy Stems from Consumer Concerns," *Journal of Young Investigators*, July 2004. www.jyi.org/volumes/volume11/issue1/features/parsley.html.
7. Parsley, "Transgenic Plants."
8. James F. Shepard, "The Regeneration of Potato Plants from Leaf-Cell Protoplasts," in *Scientific American, Understanding Cloning.* New York: Warner, 2002, p. 9.
9. Keay Davidson, "Vulnerable Farm Species," *Washington Times*, March 9, 1997.
10. Davidson, "Vulnerable Farm Species."

Chapter 2: The First Cloned Animals

11. Gina Kolata, *Clone: The Road to Dolly and the Path Ahead.* New York: William Morrow, 1998, p. 1.
12. Quoted in Arlene J. Klotzko, "Voices from Roslin: The Creators of Dolly Discuss Cloning Science, Ethics, and Social Responsibility," p. 12. www.us.oup.com/pdf/0195128 826_01.pdf.

13. Ian Wilmut et al., *The Second Creation: Dolly and the Age of Biological Control.* New York: Farrar, Straus, and Giroux, 2000, pp. 213–19.
14. Patricia Reaney, "World's First Cloned Horse Born to Its Genetic Twin," Reuters News Service, June 8, 2003, p. 1.

Chapter 3: Potential Advantages of Cloning Animals

15. Quoted in UT Cloning Project, "'Herd' the News? UT Announces 10 New Clones," October 31, 2002, p. 1. http://animalscience.ag.utk.edu/utcloneproject/news.html.
16. Quoted in UT Cloning Project, "'Herd' the News?" p. 1.
17. Quoted in UT Cloning Project, "'Herd' the News?" p. 2.
18. Quoted in UT Cloning Project, "'Herd' the News?" p. 2.
19. Wilmut et al., *The Second Creation,* p. 33.
20. Mike Adcock, report for BBC, August 21, 2003.
21. Kolata, *Clone,* p. 9.

Chapter 4: Can Cloning Save Endangered Species?

22. Biodiversity Resource Center, California Academy of Sciences, "Biodiversity Defined," 2001. www.calacademy.org/research/library/biodiv/biodiversity_defined.html.
23. Biodiversity Resource Center, "Biodiversity Defined."
24. Quoted in Jon Cohen, "Can Cloning Help Save Beleaguered Species?" *Science,* May 30, 1997, p. 42.
25. Genetic Savings and Clone, "Cat Cloning Process." www.savingsandclone.com/index2.html.
26. Rob DeSalle and David Lindley, *The Science of Jurassic Park and the Lost World, or How to Build a Dinosaur.* New York: Basic Books, 1997, pp. 57, 67–68.
27. DeSalle and Lindley, *Science of Jurassic Park and the Lost World,* pp. 89–90.

Chapter 5: The Controversial Advent of Human Cloning

28. National Bioethics Advisory Commission, *Cloning Human Beings: Report and Recommendations.* Rockville, MD, 1997, pp. 45–46.
29. International Academy of Humanism, "Declaration in Defense of Cloning," *Free Inquiry,* Summer 1997, pp. 11–12.

30. Margaret Talbot, "A Desire to Duplicate," *New York Times Magazine*, February 4, 2001, p. 41.
31. Talbot, "A Desire to Duplicate," p. 40.
32. Quoted in Human Cloning Foundation, "Father Who Has Lost His Son Favors Human Cloning." www.humancloning. org/fatherlostson.htm.
33. J.P. Lovell, "Human Cloning Is the Cure for Infertility," Human Cloning Foundation. www.humancloning.org/ infertil.php.
34. Patrick Dixon, "Future of Stem Cell Research: Rapid Progress," p. 3. www.globalchange.com/stemcells2.htm.
35. Dixon, "Future of Stem Cell Research," p. 1.
36. Rudy Baum, "Human Cloning Is Inevitable," in Paul A. Winters, ed., *Cloning*. San Diego: Greenhaven, 1998, p. 72.

Glossary

bioethics: An intellectual and literary discipline concerned with the morality of various scientific ideas and endeavors. A person involved in such work is called a bioethicist.

chromosome: A chain or string of genes.

clone: A living thing that grows from the genes of a single parent instead of two.

cystic fibrosis: A glandular disease that causes severe respiratory distress.

differentiation: The specialization of immature cells; some become skin cells, for example, while others become heart or bone marrow cells.

DNA: The major component of the genetic materials of living things.

embryo: A group of several hundred or thousand cells that grows from a fertilized egg.

embryonic: Having to do with embryos.

emphysema: A disease that impairs the healthy functioning of the lungs.

extinction: The elimination or death of a plant or animal species.

genes: Tiny particles in the cells of all living things that carry the blueprints for life.

genetic diorder: A hereditary disease caused by a defective gene passed from parent to child.

genetic donor: A living thing that provides the DNA used for cloning and other reproductive procedures.

genetic engineering: Altering one or more genes to change the physical makeup of a plant or animal.

genetic material: The DNA and other chemicals inside a cell that determine the heredity of the plant or animal of which that cell is a part.

genetics: The study of heredity.

genome: All of the genetic materials contained in a given animal or species.

hemophilia: A disease in which a person's blood does not clot properly.

heredity: The passing on of physical traits from one generation to another.

mastitis: A bacterial inflammation of cows' udders.

nucleus: The central portion of a cell, where the genetic materials are stored.

pharming: A new word meaning "the farming of drugs."

quiescence: A cell's inactive state, in which no growth or DNA replication takes place.

species: A class of plant or animal that shares common features.

sports (or **bud sports** or **somatic variants**): Plant clones that differ in some way from the parent plant.

stem cells: In an animal or human embryo, cells that have not yet differentiated, or begun to develop into specific kinds of cells (such as nerve cells or bone marrow cells).

telomere: The end of a chromosome.

transgenic animal: An animal that carries the genes of more than one species.

xenotransplant: The transplantation of an organ from a member of one species into the body of a member of another species.

For Further Reading

Books

Daniel Cohen, *Cloning*. Brookfield, CT: Millbrook, 1998. A very well-written, easy-to-understand, and interesting exploration of cloning and modern conceptions of it, aimed at general readers.

Jeanne DuPrau, *Cloning*. San Diego: Lucent, 2000. A well-organized, thorough, and informative overview of the cloning phenomenon, covering plant cloning, animal cloning, possible medical benefits of cloning, and the ethical and legal considerations of possible human cloning.

David Goodnough, *The Debate over Human Cloning*. Berkley Heights, NJ: Enslow, 2003. A good general overview of the present arguments for and against human cloning.

David Jefferis, *Cloning: Frontiers of Genetic Engineering*. New York: Crabtree, 1999. A colorfully illustrated, easy-to-read overview of the basic elements of cloning and genetic engineering.

Sally Morgan, *Body Doubles: Cloning Plants and Animals*. Crystal Lake, IL: Heinemann Library, 2003. Provides a great deal of general information on nonhuman cloning techniques and projects.

Web Sites

Cloning Ethics: Separating the Science from the Fiction (http://msnbc.msn.com/id/3076920). Noted bioethicist Arthur Caplan explains in simple terms how real cloning differs from the kind depicted in popular fiction.

Cloning Fact Sheet of the Human Genome Project (www.ornl.gov/hgmis/elsi/cloning.html). A very well-organized and informative site containing much up-to-date information about cloning, as well as links to sites with further information.

Cloning Information at NewScientist.com (www.new scientist.com/hottopics/cloning). Contains many frequently updated links to articles and photos about various aspects of cloning.

Genetic Savings and Clone (www.savingsandclone.com/ index2.html). This site, provided by a company that has already cloned pet cats, explains the company's methods and goals.

Human Cloning Foundation (www.humancloning.org). This organization advocates research into human cloning, which it claims will benefit, rather than harm, human society.

Clonaid (www.clonaid.com). The Raelians, who believe that the entire human race was cloned by aliens, claim to have cloned humans, although thus far they have produced no definitive proof.

Works Consulted

MAJOR WORKS

Lori B. Andrews, *The Clone Age: Adventures in the New World of Reproductive Technology.* New York: Henry Holt, 1999. An excellent overview of the cloning phenomenon and related topics.

Jose B. Cibelli, Robert P. Lanza, Keith Campbell, and Michael D. West, *Principles of Cloning.* San Diego: Academic Press, 2002. A large, scholarly, up-to-date study of the subject put together by a number of scholars involved in cloning research.

Rob DeSalle and David Lindley, *The Science of Jurassic Park and the Lost World, or How to Build a Dinosaur.* New York: Basic Books, 1997. A brilliant and fascinating look at the scientific technology and possibilities involved in the cloning of extinct animal species.

Leon R. Kass and James Q. Wilson, *The Ethics of Human Cloning.* Washington, DC: AEI, 1998. This is a thoughtful, well-informed view of some of the ethical and moral concerns surrounding cloning, including how such cloning technology and its products might affect the family.

Gina Kolata, *Clone: The Road to Dolly and the Path Ahead.* New York: William Morrow, 1998. Kolata, a noted science writer for the *New York Times*, delivers an informative, thought-provoking summary of the various scientific discoveries, attitudes, and debates related to cloning before Dolly the sheep became the first animal clone in 1996.

Paul Lauritzen, *Cloning and the Future of Human Embryo Research.* New York: Oxford University Press, 2001. A well-balanced summary of present knowledge about cloning humans and the real possibility that such technology will soon be used to create human clones.

Jane Maeenschein, *Whose View of Life? Embryos, Cloning, and Stem Cells.* Cambridge, MA: Harvard University Press, 2003.

A fine overview of current research regarding stem cells and cloning.

Gregory I. Pence, *Cloning After Dolly: Who's Still Afraid?* Lanham, MD: Rowman and Littlefield, 2005. A controversial but excellent new examination of the cloning debate; the author argues that all forms of cloning should be made legal rather than banned.

Scientific American, Understanding Cloning. New York: Warner, 2002. A useful collection of essays (most of them scholarly) on cloning and related topics.

Lee M. Silver, *Remaking Eden: Cloning and Beyond in a Brave New World.* New York: Avon, 1997. One of the better recent books about cloning. Covers in vitro fertilization; parental questions raised by cloning; the possibility of designer children; and much more.

Jon Turney, *Frankenstein's Footsteps: Science, Genetics, and Popular Culture.* New Haven, CT: Yale University Press, 1998. A brisk exploration of changing public attitudes about cloning and the way the public often fears or sees a distorted image of science and its newer, more controversial creations.

Ian Wilmut, Keith Campbell, and Colin Tudge, *The Second Creation: Dolly and the Age of Biological Control.* New York: Farrar, Straus, and Giroux, 2000. The researchers who cloned Dolly in 1996 explain their initial goals, their experiments, how they made Dolly, and the possible implications of their work. An important document in cloning literature.

OTHER IMPORTANT WORKS

Books

Barbara MacKinnon, ed., *Human Cloning: Science, Ethics, and Public Policy.* Champaign: University of Illinois Press, 2000.

Charles C. Mann and Mark L. Plummer, *Noah's Choice: The Future of Endangered Species:* New York: Knopf, 1995.

Gary E. McCuen, ed., *Cloning: Science and Society.* Hudson, WI: Gary E. McCuen, 1998.

Lynn Messina, ed., *Biotechnology.* New York: H.W. Wilson, 2000.

Martha C. Nussbaum and Cass R. Sunstein, eds., *Clones and Clones: Facts and Fantasies About Human Cloning.* New York: W.W. Norton, 1998.

Paul A. Winters, ed., *Cloning.* San Diego: Greenhaven, 1998.

Lisa Yount, ed., *Cloning*. San Diego: Greenhaven, 2000.

Articles, Reports, and Letters

Mike Adcock, report for BBC, August 21, 2003.

Gary B. Anderson and George E. Seidel, "Cloning for Profit," *Science*, May 29, 1998.

Jon Cohen, "Can Cloning Help Save Beleaguered Species?" *Science*, May 30, 1997.

Keay Davidson, "Vulnerable Farm Species," *Washington Times*, March 9, 1997.

Wray Herbert et al., "The World After Cloning," *U.S. News & World Report*, March 10, 1997.

International Academy of Humanism, "Declaration in Defense of Cloning," *Free Inquiry*, Summer 1997.

Jeffrey Kluger, "Will We Follow the Sheep?" *Time*, March 10, 1997.

Gina Kolata, "Researchers Find Big Risk of Defect in Cloning Animals," *New York Times*, March 25, 2001.

Ruth Macklin, "Human Cloning? Don't Just Say No," *U.S. News & World Report*, March 10, 1997.

Jay Maeder, "Bring 'em Back Alive," *U.S. News & World Report*, October 13, 1997.

Michael Mautner, "Will Cloning End Human Evolution?" *Futurist*, November/December 1997.

National Bioethics Advisory Commission, *Cloning Human Beings: Report and Recommendations*. Rockville, MD, 1997.

Elizabeth Pennisi, "After Dolly, a Pharming Frenzy," *Science*, January 30, 1998.

———, "Cloned Mice Provide Company for Dolly," *Science*, July 24, 1998.

Patricia Reaney, "World's First Cloned Horse Born to Its Genetic Twin," Reuters News Service, June 8, 2003.

Jeremy Rifkin, "Future Pharming—Genetic Engineering of Animals," *Animals*, May/June 1998.

"Statement of Senator Edward M. Kennedy," Hearing on Cloning, *Congressional Record*, March 5, 2002.

Richard Stone, "Cloning the Woolly Mammoth," *Discover*, April 1999.

Margaret Talbot, "A Desire to Duplicate," *New York Times Magazine*, February 4, 2001.

Alan Taylor, "Silence of the Lamb," *New Yorker*, March 17, 1997.

Ian Wilmut et al., "Viable Offspring Derived from Fetal and Adult Mammalian Cells," *Nature*, February 27, 1997.

Panayiotis Zavos, letter in the *Sunday Herald*, Edinburgh, Scotland, October 21, 2001.

Internet Sources

Biodiversity Resource Center, California Academy of Sciences, "Biodiversity Defined," 2001. www.calacademy.org/re search/ library/biodiv/biodiversity_defined.html.

Common Ground, "Richard Cox and the Cox's Orange Pippin." www.england-in-particular.info/cox.html.

Patrick Dixon, "Future of Stem Cell Research: Rapid Progress." www.globalchange.com/stemcells2.htm.

Greenpeace, "Invasion of the Forest Snatchers," January 20, 2005. www.greenpeace.org/international/news/invasion-of-the-forest-snatcher.

Human Cloning Foundation, "Father Who Has Lost His Son Favors Human Cloning." www.humancloning.org/father lostson.htm.

Arlene J. Klotzko, "Voices from Roslin: The Creators of Dolly Discuss Cloning Science, Ethics, and Social Responsibility." www.us.oup.com/pdf/0195128826_01.pdf.

Will Knight, "First Cloned Pet Revives Ethical Debate," NewScientist.com, December 23, 2004. www.newscientist. com/article.ns?id=dn6833.

J.P. Lovell, "Human Cloning Is the Cure for Infertility," Human Cloning Foundation. www.humancloning.org/infertil.php.

Larissa Parsley, "Transgenic Plants: A Budding Controversy Stems from Consumer Concerns," *Journal of Young Investigators,* July 2004. www.jyi.org/volumes/volume11/ issue1/features/parsley.html.

Phytocultures Ltd., "Other Plants: An Overview," 2004. www.phytocultures.com/other_overview.asp.

Simon Smith, "The Benefits of Human Cloning," Human Cloning Foundation, 2002. www.humancloning.org/benefits.php.

Bijal P. Trivedi, "Grasshoppers Used to Fight 'Worst Water Weed,'" *National Geographic,* April 1, 2003. http://news.national geographic.com/news/2003/04/0401_030401_tvhyacinth. html.

UT Cloning Project, "'Herd' the News? UT Announces 10 New Clones," October 31, 2002. http://animalscience.ag.utk. edu/utcloneproject/news.html.

Index

Picture Credits

About the Author

In addition to his acclaimed volumes on ancient civilizations, historian Don Nardo has published several studies of modern scientific discoveries and phenomena. In addition to *Cloning*, these include *Black Holes; Extraterrestrial Life; Atoms; Gravity; The Extinction of the Dinosaurs;* volumes about Pluto, Neptune, and the moon; and a biography of the noted scientist Charles Darwin. Mr. Nardo lives with his wife, Christine, in Massachusetts.